George William Foote

Flowers of freethought

George William Foote

Flowers of freethought

ISBN/EAN: 9783337112059

Printed in Europe, USA, Canada, Australia, Japan

Cover: Foto ©ninafisch / pixelio.de

More available books at **www.hansebooks.com**

FLOWERS

OF

FREETHOUGHT

BY

G. W. FOOTE.

LONDON:
R. FORDER, 28 STONECUTTER STREET, E.C.

1893.

LONDON:
PRINTED AND PUBLISHED BY G. W. FOOTE,
AT 14 CLERKENWELL GREEN, E.C.

PREFACE.

HEINRICH HEINE called himself a soldier in the army of human liberation. It was a modest description of himself, for he was more; his position was that of a leader, and his sword was like the mystic Excalibur, flashing with the hues of his genius, and dealing death to the enemies of freedom.

Humbler fighters than Heine may count themselves as simple soldiers in that great army, whose leaders' names are graven deep in the history of modern Europe. I also venture to rank myself with them, and it is the summit of my ambition. To be indeed a soldier in that army, however low and obscure, is not to have lived in vain; to persevere, to fight to the end, is to live (if unknown) in the future of humanity.

In the course of my service to "the cause" I have wielded tongue and pen as weapons. The spoken word has gone, like spilt water, except as it may have made an impression on the listeners. The written word remains. Most of it, in truth, was only the week's work, done honestly, but under no special impulse. Some of the rest—as I have been told, and as in a few cases I feel—is of less doubtful value; having occasionally the merit of a free play of mind on subjects that are too often treated with ignorance, timidity, or hypocrisy.

This is my reason for publishing in a separate and durable form the articles in this collection. Whether it is a sufficient reason the reader will judge for himself.

No serious attempt has been made at classification. Here and there articles have been placed in intended proximity, though written at different intervals in the past ten years. Sometimes, for an obvious reason, the date of composition has been indicated. Otherwise there is no approach to systematic arrangement; and if this is a defect, the reader has on the other hand the benefit of variety.

The ambitious, and hardly execusable, thing about this collection is its title. But the selection of a label for such a miscellany was not an easy task, and I ask the reader's indulgence in consideration of the difficulty. The title I have chosen is at least a pretty one, and in a sense it is appropriate. These articles are flowers of *my* Freethought; the blossomings of my mind on particular occasions, after much investigation and pondering.

Wherever I have made a rash statement I shall be happy to be corrected; wherever I may have argued wrongly, I shall be happy to be set right. But I am less amenable to appeals on the ground of "taste." They are almost invariably made by those who wish failure to one's propaganda. A fair controversialist will refrain from personalities. I have done this, and I will do no more. I believe in free thought and honest speech. In the war of ideas there is neither treaty nor truce. To ask for quarter is to admit defeat; and to give it is treachery to Truth.

April, 1893.   G. W. FOOTE.

CONTENTS.

	PAGE
Old Nick	1
Fire !!!	7
Sky Pilots	11
Devil Dodgers	15
Fighting Spooks	19
Damned Sinners	22
Where is Hell?	27
Spurgeon and Hell	30
Is Spurgeon in Heaven?	34
God in Japan	38
Stanley on Providence	42
Gone to God	45
Thank God	49
Judgment Day	52
Shelley's Atheism	61
Long Faces	71

	PAGE
Our Father	77
Wait Till You Die	81
Dead Theology	84
Mr. Gladstone on Devils	94
Huxley's Mistake	97
The Gospel of Freethought	101
On Ridicule	108
Who are the Blasphemers?	112
Christianity and Common Sense	114
The Lord of Lords	117
Consecrating the Colors	122
Christmas in Holloway Gaol	125
Who Killed Christ?	130
Did Jesus Ascend?	134
The Rising Son	137
St. Paul's Veracity	140
No Faith with Heretics	145
The Logic of Persecution	147
Luther and the Devil	151
Bible English	157
Living by Faith	161
Victor Hugo	163

	PAGE
Desecrating a Church	166
Walt Whitman	169
Tennyson and the Bible	174
Christ's Old Coat	179
Christ's Coat, Number Two	183
Scotched, Not Slain	186
God-Making	189
God and the Weather	193
Miracles	196
A Real Miracle	200
Jesus on Women	204
Paul on Women	208
Mother's Religion	212

OLD NICK.

THIS gentleman is of very ancient descent. His lineage dwarfs that of the proudest nobles and kings. English peers whose ancestors came in with the Conqueror; the Guelphs, Hapsburgs, and Hohenzollerns of our European thrones; are things of yesterday compared with his Highness the Devil. The Cæsars themselves, the more ancient rulers of Assyria, and even the Pharaohs of the first dynasty, are modern beside him. His origin is lost in the impenetrable obscurity of primitive times. Nay, there have been sages who maintained his eternity, who made him coeval with God, and placed upon his head the crown of a divided sovereignty of the infinite universe.

But time and change are lords of all, and the most durable things come to an end. Celestial and infernal, like earthly, powers are subject to the law of decay. Mutability touches them with her dissolving wand, and strong necessity, the lord of gods and men, brings them to the inevitable stroke of Death. Senility falls on all beings and institutions—if they are allowed to perish naturally; and as our august Monarchy is the joke of wits, and our ancient House of Lords is an object of popular derision, so the high and mighty Devil in his palsied old age is the laughing-stock of those who once trembled at the sound of his name. They omit the lofty titles he was once addressed by, and fearless of his feeble thunders and lightnings, they familiarly style him Old Nick. Alas, how are the mighty fallen! The potentate who was more terrible than an army with banners is now the sport of children and a common figure in melodrama. Even the genius of Milton, Goethe, and Byron, has not been able to save him from this miserable fate.

When this sobriquet of Old Nick first came into use is unknown. Macaulay, in his essay on Machiavelli, says that "Out of his surname they have coined an epithet for a knave, and out of his Christian name a synonym for the Devil." A couplet from *Hudibras* is cited to support this view.

> Nick Machiavel had ne'er a trick
> Tho' he gave his name to our Old Nick.

"But we believe," adds Macaulay, "there is a schism on this subject among the antiquaries." The learned Zachary Gray's edition of *Hudibras* shows that "our English writers, before Machiavel's time, used the word Old Nick very commonly to signify the Devil," and that "it came from our Saxon ancestors, who called him Old Nicka." No doubt Butler, whose learning was so great that he "knew everything," was well acquainted with this fact. He probably meant the couplet as a broad stroke of humor. But there was perhaps a chronological basis for the joke. Our Saxon ancestors did not speak of Old Nicka in a spirit of jest or levity. The bantering sense of our modern sobriquet for the Devil appears to have crept in during the decline of witchcraft. That frightful saturnalia of superstition was the Devil's heyday. He was almost omnipotent and omnipresent. But as witchcraft died out, partly through the growth of knowledge, and partly through sheer weariness on the part of its devotees, the Devil began to lose his power. His agency in human affairs was seen to be less potent than was imagined. People called him Old Nick playfully, as they might talk of a toothless old mastiff whose bark was worse than his bite. At length he was regarded as a perfect fraud, and his sobriquet took a tinge of contempt. He is now utterly played out except in church and chapel, where the sky-pilots still represent him as a roaring lion. Yet, as a curious relic of old times, it may be noted that in the law-courts, where conservatism reigns in the cumbrous wig on the judge's head, and in the cumbrous phraseology of indictments, criminals are still charged with being instigated by the Devil. Nearly all the judges look upon this as so much nonsense, but occasionally there is a pious fossil who treats it seriously. We then hear a Judge North regret that a prisoner has devoted the abilities God gave him to the Devil's service, and give the renegade a year's leisure to reconsider which master he ought to serve.

During the witch mania the world was treated to a great deal of curious information about Old Nick. What Robert Burns says of him in *Tam O'Shanter* is only a faint reminiscence of the wealth of demonology which existed a few generations earlier. Old Nick used to appear at the witches' Sabbaths in the form of a goat, or a brawny black man, who courted all the pretty young witches and made them submit to his embraces. Some of these crazy creatures, under examination or torture, gave the most circumstantial accounts of their intercourse with Satan; their revelations being of such an obscene character that they must be left under the veil of a dead tongue. It is, of course, absurd to suppose that anything of the kind occurred. Religious hysteria and lubricity are closely allied, as every physician knows, and the filthy fancies of a lively witch deserve no more attention than those of many females in our lunatic asylums.

Behind these tales of the Devil there was the pagan tradition of Pan, whose upper part was that of a man and his lower part that of a goat. The devils of one religion are generally the gods of its predecessor; and the great Pan, whose myth is so beautifully expounded by Bacon, was degraded by Christianity into a fiend. Representing, as he did, the nature which Christianity trampled under foot, he became a fit incarnation of the Devil. The horns and hooves and the goat thighs were preserved; and the emblems of strength, fecundity and wisdom in the god became the emblems of bestiality and cunning in the demon.

Heine's magnificent *Gods in Exile* shows how the

deities of Olympus avenged themselves for this illtreatment. They haunted the mountains and forests, beguiling knights and travellers from their allegiance to Christ. Venus wooed the men who were taught by an ascetic creed to despise sexual love; and Pan, appearing as the Devil, led the women a frightful dance to hell.

But as the Christian superstition declined, the gods of Paganism also disappeared. Their vengeance was completed, and they retired with the knowledge that the gods of Calvary were mortal like the gods of Olympus.

During the last two centuries the Devil has gradually become a subject for joking. In Shakespeare's plays he is still a serious personage, although we fancy that the mighty bard had no belief himself in any such being. But, as a dramatist, he was obliged to suit himself to the current fashion of thought, and he refers to the Devil when it serves his purpose just as he introduces ghosts and witches. His Satanic Majesty not being then a comic figure, he is spoken of or alluded to with gravity. Even when Macbeth flies at the messenger in a towering rage, and cries "the Devil damn thee black, thou cream-faced loon," he does not lose his sense of the Devil's dignity. In Milton's great epic Satan is really the central figure, and he is always splendid and heroic. Shelley, in fact, complained in his preface to *Prometheus Unbound* that "the character of Satan engenders in the mind a pernicious casuistry, which leads us to weigh his faults with his wrongs, and to excuse the former because the latter exceed all measure." Goethe's Mephistopheles is less dignified than Milton's Satan, but he is full of energy and intellect, and if Faust eventually escapes from his clutches it is only by a miracle. At any rate, Mephistopheles is not an object of derision; on the contrary, the laugh is generally on his own side. Still, Goethe is playing with the Devil all the time. He does not believe in the actual existence of the Prince of Evil, but simply uses the familiar old figure to work out a psychological drama. The same is true of Byron. Satan, in the *Vision of Judgment*, is a superb presence, moving with a princely splendor; but had it suited his purpose, Byron could have made him a very different character.

The Devil is, indeed, treated with much greater levity by Coleridge and Southey, and Shelley knocks him about a good deal in *Peter Bell the Third*—

> The Devil, I safely can aver,
> Has neither hoof, nor tail, nor sting;
> Nor is he, as some sages swear,
> A spirit, neither here nor there,
> In nothing—yet in everything.
>
> He is—what we are! for sometimes
> The Devil is a gentleman;
> At others a bard bartering rhymes
> For sack; a statesman spinning crimes;
> A swindler, living as he can.

These and many other verses show what liberties Shelley took with the once formidable monarch of hell.

The Devil's treatment by the pulpiteers is instructive. Take up an old sermon and you will find the Devil all over it. The smell of brimstone is on every page, and you see the whisk of his tail as you turn the leaf. But things are changed now. Satan is no longer a person, except in the vulgar circles of sheer illiteracy, where the preacher is as great an ignoramus as his congregation. If you take up any reputable volume of sermons by a Church parson or a Dissenting minister, you find the Devil either takes a back seat or disappears altogether in a metaphysical cloud. None of these subtle resolvers of ancient riddles, however, approaches grand old Donne, who said in one of his fine discourses that "the Devil himself is only concentrated stupidity." What a magnificent flash of insight! Yes, the great enemy of mankind is stupidity; and, alas, against that, as Schiller said, the gods themselves fight in vain. Yet time fights against it, and time is greater than the gods; so there is hope after all.

Gradually the Devil has dropped, until he has at last reached the lowest depth. He is now patronised by the Salvation Army. Booth exhibits him for a living, and all the Salvation Army Captains and Hallelujah Lasses parade him about to the terror of a few fools and the amusement of everyone else. Poor Devil! Belisarius begging an obolus was nothing to this. Surely the Lord himself might take pity on his old rival, and assist him out of this miserable plight.

Old Nick is now used to frighten children with, and by-and-bye he may be employed like the old garden-god to frighten away the crows. Even his scriptural reputation cannot save him from such a fate, for the Bible itself is falling into disbelief and contempt, and his adventures from Genesis to Revelation are become a subject of merriment. Talking to Mrs. Eve about apples in the form of a serpent; whispering in David's ear that a census would be a good thing, while Jehovah whispers a similar suggestion on the other side; asking Jesus to turn pebbles into penny loaves, lugging him through the air, perching him on a pinnacle, setting him on the top of a mountain whence both squinted round the globe, and playing for forty days and nights that preposterous pantomime of the temptation in the desert; getting miraculously multiplied, bewildering a herd of swine, and driving them into a watery grave; letting seven of himself occupy one lady called Magdalen, and others inhabit the bodies of lunatics; going about like a roaring lion, and then appearing in the new part of a dragon who lashes the stars with his tail; all these metamorphoses are ineffably ludicrous, and calculated to excite inextinguishable laughter. His one serious appearance in the history of Job is overwhelmed by this multitude of comic situations.

Poor Old Nick is on his last legs and cannot last much longer. May his end be peace! That is the least we can wish him. And when he is dead, let us hope he will receive a decent burial. Those to whom he has been the best friend should follow him to the grave. His obsequies, in that case, would be graced by the presence of all the clergy, and the Burial Service might be read by the Archbishop of Canterbury. Fancy them, burying their dear departed brother the Devil, in the sure and certain hope of a glorious resurrection!

FIRE!!!

Do not be alarmed, dear reader; there is no need to rush out into the street, like poor old Lot flying from the doomed Cities of the Plain. Sit down and take it easy. Let your fire-insurance policy slumber in its nest. Lean back in your chair, stretch out your legs, and prepare to receive another dose of Freethought physic—worth a guinea a bottle. So! Are you ready? Very well then, let us begin.

What would man be without fire? Would he not be a perfect barbarian? His very food, even the meat, would have to be eaten raw, and as knives and forks would be unknown, it would have to be devoured with hands and teeth. We read that the Tartar horseman will put a beefsteak under his saddle, and supple and cook it in a ten-mile ride; but we cannot all follow his example, and many would think the game was not worth the candle. But not only should we be obliged to eat our food uncooked; we should enjoy none of the blessings and comforts bestowed upon us by science, which absolutely depends on fire. Nay, our houses would be too cold to shelter us in the winter, and we should be compelled to burrow in the ground. The whole human race would have to live in tropical countries; all the temperate regions would be deserted; and as it is in the temperate regions that civilisation reaches its highest and most permanent developments, the world would be reduced to a condition of barbarism if not of savagery.

No wonder, then, that this mighty civiliser has figured so extensively in legend and mythology. "Next to the worship of the sun," says Max Müller, "there is probably no religious worship so widely diffused as that of Fire." At bottom, indeed, the two were nearly identical. The flame of burning wood was felt to be akin to the rays of the sun, and its very upward motion seemed an aspiration to its source. Sun and fire alike gave warmth, which meant life and joy; without them there reigned sterility and death. Do we not still speak of the *sunshine* of prosperity, and of basking in the *rays* of fortune? Do we not still speak of the *fire* of life, of inspiration, of love, of heroism? And thus when the tide of our being is at the flood, we instinctively think of our father the Sun, in whom, far more than in invisible gods, we live and move—for we are all his children.

Like everything else in civilised existence, fire was a human discovery. But superstitious ages imagined that so precious a thing must have descended from above. Accordingly the Greeks (to take but one illustration) fabled that Prometheus stole Jove's fire from Heaven and gave it to mankind. And as the gods of early ages are not too friendly to human beings, it was also fabled that Prometheus incurred the fierce anger of Jove, who fastened him to a rock on Mount Caucasus, where he was blistered by day and frozen by night, while Jove's vulture everlastingly preyed upon his vitals.

The sun himself, in oriental countries, shining down implacably in times of prolonged drought, became a terrible demon, and as Baal or Moloch was worshipped with cruel and bloody rites. The corruption of the best is the worst; beneficence changes to malignity. Thus fire, which is a splendid servant, is an awful master. The very wild beasts dread it. Famishing lions and tigers will not approach the camp-fire to seize their prey. Men have something of the same instinctive apprehension. How soon the nerves are disturbed by the smell of anything burning in the house. Raise the cry of "Fire!" in a crowded building, and at once the old savage bursts through the veneer of civilisation. It is helter-skelter, the Devil take the hindmost. The strong trample upon the weak. Men and women turn to devils. Even if the cry of "Fire!" be raised in a church—where a believer might wish to die, and where he might feel himself booked through to glory—there is just the same stampede. People who sit and listen complacently to the story of eternal roastings in an everlasting hell, will fight like maniacs to escape a singeing. Rather than go to heaven in a chariot of fire they will plod for half a century in this miserable vale of tears.

Man's dread of fire has been artfully seized upon by the priests. All over the world these gentlemen are in the same line of business—trading upon the credulous terrors of the multitude. They fill Hell with fire, because it frightens men easily, and the fuel costs nothing. If they had to find the fuel themselves Hell would be cold in twenty-four hours. "Flee from the wrath to come," they exclaim. "What is it?" ask the people. "Consuming fire," the priests exclaim, "nay, not consuming; you will burn in it without dying, without losing a particle of flesh, for ever and ever." Then the people want to get saved, and the priests issue insurance policies, which are rendered void by change of opinion or failure to pay the premium.

Buddhist pictures of hell teach the eye the same lesson that is taught the ear by Christian sermons.

There are the poor damned wretches rolling in the fire; there are the devils shovelling in fuel, and other devils with long toasting-forks thrusting back the victims that shove their noses out of the flames.

Wherever the priests retain their old power over the people's minds they still preach a hell of literal fire, and deliver twenty sermons on Hades to one on Paradise. Hell, in fact, is always as hot as the people will stand it. The priests reduce the temperature with natural reluctance. Every degree lost is a sinking of their power and profit.

Even in England—the land of Shakespeare and Shelley, Newton and Darwin, Mill and Spencer—the cry of "Fire!" is still raised in thousands of pulpits. Catholics bate no jot of their fiery damnation; Church of England clergymen hold forth on brimstone—with now and then a dash of treacle—in the rural districts and small towns; it is not long since the Wesleyans turned out a minister who was not cocksure about everlasting torment; Mr. Spurgeon preaches hell (hot, without sugar) in mercy to perishing souls; and General Booth, who caters for the silliest and most ignorant Christians, works hell into his trade-mark.

"Blood and Fire" is a splendid summary of the orthodox faith. All who would be saved must be washed in the Blood of the Lamb—a disgusting ablution! All who are not saved fall into the Fire. A blood-bath or a sulphur-bath is the only alternative.

Happily, however, the people are becoming more civilised and more humane. Science and popular education are working wonders. Reason, self-reliance, and sympathy are rapidly developing. The old primitive terrors are losing their hold upon us, and the callous dogmas of savage religion are growing impossible. Priests cannot frighten men who possess a high sense of human dignity; and the doctrine of an angry God, who will burn his own children in hell, is loathsome to those who will fight the flames and smoke of a burning house to save the life of an unknown fellow creature.

How amusing, in these circumstances, are the wrigglings of the "advanced" Christians. Archdeacon Farrar, for instance, in despite of common sense and etymology, contends that "everlasting" fire only means "eternal" fire. What a comfort the distinction would be to a man in Hell! Away with such temporising! Let the ghastly old dogma be defied. Sensible people should simply laugh at the priests who still raise the cry of "Fire!"

SKY PILOTS.

THE authorship of the designation "sky pilot" is as unknown as that of the four gospels. Yet its origin is recent. It has only been in use for a few years, say ten, or at the outside twenty. Nobody knows, however, who was the first man from whose lips it fell. Probably he was an American, but his name and address are not ascertained. Surely this fact, which has thousands if not millions of parallels, should abate the impudence of religionists who ask "Who made the world?" when they do not know who made nine-tenths of the well-known things it contains.

Whatever its origin, the designation is a happy one. It fits like a glove. Repeat it to the first man you meet, and though he never heard it before, he will know that you mean a minister. For this very reason it makes the men of God angry. They feel insulted, and let you see it. They accuse you of calling them names, and if you smile too sarcastically they will indulge in some well-selected Bible language themselves.

There are some trades that will not bear honest designations, and the minister's is one of them. Call him what you please, except what he is, and he is not disquieted. But call him "sky-pilot" and he starts up like Macbeth at the ghost of Banquo, exclaiming "Come in any other form but that!"

Go down to the seaside and look at one of those bluff, weather-beaten, honest fellows, who know all the rocks and shoals, and tides and channels, for miles around. Call one of them a "pilot," and he will not be offended. The term is legitimate. It exactly denotes his business. He is rather proud of it. His calling is honorable and useful. He pilots ships through uncertain and dangerous waters to their destination. He does his work, takes his pay, and feels satisfied; and if you cry "pilot!" he answers merrily with a "what cheer?"

But "sky" in front of "pilot" makes all the difference. It makes the man of God feel like having a cold shower bath; then the reaction sets in and he grows hot—sometimes as hot as H——well, Hades. We are not going to swear if the parson does.

But after all, he *is* a "pilot" and a "sky" pilot. He undertakes to pilot people to Heaven. Let him board your ship and take the helm, and he will guide you over the Black Sea of Death to Port Felicity. That, at least, is what he says in his trade circular, though it turns out very differently in practice, as we shall see presently.

Let us first notice a great difference between the sea pilot and the sky pilot. The honest salt boards the ship, and takes her out to sea, or brings her into port. When the work is over he presents his bill, or it is done for him. He does not ask for payment in advance. He neither takes nor gives credit. But the sky pilot does take credit and he gives none. He is always paid beforehand. Every year he expects a good retaining fee in the shape of a stipend or a benefice, or a good percentage of the pew rents and collections. But when his services are really wanted he leaves you in the lurch. You do not need a pilot to Heaven until you come to die. Then your voyage begins in real earnest. But the sky-pilot does not go with you. Oh dear no! That is no part of *his* bargain. "Ah my friend," he says, "I must leave you now. You must do the rest for yourself. I have coached you for years in celestial navigation; if you remember my lessons you will have a prosperous voyage. Good day, dear friend. I'm going to see another customer. But we shall meet again."

Now this is not a fair contract. It is really obtaining money under false pretences. The sky pilot has never been to Heaven himself. He does not know the way. Anyhow, there are hundreds of different routes, and they cannot all lead to the same place. Certainly they all start from this world, but that is all they have in common, and where they end is a puzzle. To pay money in such circumstances is foolish and an encouragement to fraud. The best way to pay for goods is on delivery; in the same way the sky pilot should be paid at the finish.

But how is that to be done? Well, easily. All you have to do is to address the sky pilot in this fashion —"Dearly beloved pilot to the land of bliss! let our contract be fair and mutual. Give me credit as I give you credit. Don't ask for cash on account. I'll pay at the finish. Your directions may be sound; they ought to be, for you are very dogmatic. Still, there is room for doubt, and I don't want to be diddled. You tell me to follow your rules of celestial navigation. Well, I will. You say we shall meet at Port Felicity. Well, I hope so; and when we do meet I'll square up."

Of course, it may be objected that this would starve the sky pilots. But why should it do anything of the kind? Have *they* no faith? Must all the faith be on *our* side? Should they not practise a little of what they preach? God tells them to *pray* for their daily bread, and no doubt he would add some cheese and butter. All they have to do is to *ask* for it. "Ask and ye shall receive," says the text, and it has many confirmations. For forty years the Jews were among the unemployed, and Jehovah sent them food daily. "He rained down bread from heaven." The prophet Elijah, also, lived in the wilderness on the sandwiches God sent him—bread and meat in the morning, and bread and meat in the evening. There was likewise the widow's cruse of oil and barrel of flour, which supported her and the man of God day by day without diminishing. These things actually happened. They are as true as the Bible. And they may happen again. At any rate they *should* happen. The sky-pilots should subsist on the fruits of prayer. Let them live by faith—not *our* faith, but *their* own. This will prove their sincerity, and give us some trust in their teaching. And if they *should* starve in the experiment—well, it is worth making, and they will fall martyrs to truth and human happiness. *One* batch of martyrs will suffice. There will be no need of what Gibbon calls "an annual consumption."

The men of God pilot *us* to Heaven, but they are very loth to go there themselves. Heaven is their "home," but they prefer exile, even in this miserable vale of tears. When they fall ill, they do not welcome it as a call from the Father. They do not sing "Nearer my God to thee." We do not find them going about saying "I shall be home shortly." Oh no! They indulge freely in self-pity. Like a limpet to a rock do they cling to this wretched, sinful world. Congregations are asked if they cannot "do something," a subscription is got up, and the man of God rushes off to the seaside, where prayer, in co-operation with oxygen and ozone, restore him to health, enable him to dodge "going home," and qualify him for another term of penal servitude on earth.

It appears to us that sky pilots, like other men, should be judged by their practice. If they show no belief in what they preach, we are foolish to believe in it any more than they do. It also appears to us that their profession is as fraudulent as fortune-telling. Many a poor old woman has been imprisoned for taking sixpence from a servant girl, after promising her a tall, dark husband and eight fine children; but men dressed in black coats and white chokers are allowed to take money for promises of good fortune in the "beautiful land above." It further appears to us that the sky pilots should be compelled to come to a reasonable agreement before their trade is licensed. They should settle *where Heaven is* before they begin business. Better still, perhaps, every applicant for a license should prove that *some* human soul *has been* piloted to Heaven. Until that is done, the profession is only robbery and imposture.

DEVIL DODGERS.

MOST people suppose this phrase to be a recent Americanism. It occurs, however, in the Memoirs of James Lackington, published in 1791. Speaking of certain ranting preachers, he says—"These *devil-dodgers* happened to be so very powerful that they soon sent John home, crying out, that he should be damned."

Admitting the age of the phrase, some will ask, Is it respectable? Well, that is a matter of taste. Is there any standard of respectability? Does it not vary with time, place, and circumstance? Some people hate wearing gloves, while other people feel half naked without them. A box hat is a great sign of respectability; when a vestryman wears one he overawes philosophers; yet some men would as soon wear the helmet of Don Quixote. Flannel suits are quite shocking in town; at the seaside they are the height of fashion. And as it is with dress so it is with speech. The "respectable" classes are apt to rob language of its savor, clipping and trimming it like the trees in a Dutch garden. You must go to the common, unrespectable classes for racy vigor of tongue. They avoid circumlocutions, eschew diffuseness, go straight to the point, and prefer concrete to abstract expressions. They don't speak of a foolish man, they call him a fool; a cowardly talebearer they call a sneak; and so on to the end of the chapter. But is this really vulgar? Open your Shakespeare, or any other dramatic poet, and you will find it is not so. A look, a gesture, is more expressive than words; and concrete language carries more weight than the biggest abstractions.

Let us break up the phrase, and see where the "vulgarity" comes in. There is nothing vulgar about the Devil. He is reputed to be a highly-accomplished gentleman. Milton, Goethe, and Byron have even felt his grandeur. And is not "dodger" clear as well as expressive? David dodged Saul's javelin. That was smart and proper. Afterwards he attempted a dodge on Uriah. That was mean and dirty. So that "dodge" may be good, bad, or indifferent, like "man" or "woman." There is nothing objectionable about it *per se*. And if "devil" and "dodger" are respectable in their single state, how do they become vulgar when they are married?

Of course it is quite natural for the clergy and their thorough-paced dupes to cry out against plain language. The clerical trade is founded on mystery, and "behind every mystery there is a cheat." Calling things by their right names will always be ugly to impostors.

"Reverend" sounds so much nicer than "mystery-man," "priest" is more dignified than "fortune-teller," "clergyman" is pleasanter than "sky-pilot," and "minister" is more soothing than "devil-dodger." But plain speech is always wholesome if you keep within the bounds of truth. It does us good to see ourselves occasionally as others see us. And if this article should fall under the eyes of a Christian man of God, we beg him to keep his temper and read on to the end.

We tell the men of God, of every denomination, that they are Devil Dodgers, and when they cease to be that their occupation is going. Old Nick, in some form or other, is the basis of every kind of Christianity. Indeed, the dread of evil, the terror of calamity, is at the bottom of all religion; while the science which gives us foresight and power, and enables us to protect ourselves and promote our comfort, is religion's deadliest enemy. Science wars against evil practically; religion wars against it theoretically. Science sees the material causes that are at work, and counteracts them; religion is too lazy and conceited to study the causes, it takes the evil in a lump, personifies it, and christens it " the Devil." Thus it keeps men off the real path of deliverance, and teaches them to fear the Bogie-Man, who is simply a phantom of superstition, and always vanishes at the first forward step of courage.

What is the Christian scheme in a nutshell? God made man perfect—though some people, after reading the life of Adam, say that God made him a perfect fool. This perfect man was tackled by the Devil, a sort of spiritual Pasteur, who inoculated him with sin, which was transmitted to his posterity as *original* sin. God desires man's welfare, but the Devil is too strong for Omnipotence. Jesus Christ steps in with the Holy Ghost and saves a few men and women, but the Devil bags all the rest, and Hell is thronged while Heaven is half empty; the one place having three families on every flat, the other having leagues of spacious mansions " to let."

Now in every generation the Devil is after us. Without schools, or churches, or armies of professional helpers, or even so much as an occasional collection, he carries on single-handed a most successful business. The clergy tell us, as the Bible tells them, that he is monstrously able, active and enterprising; never overlooking a single customer, and delivering damnation at the door, and even carrying it upstairs, without charging for carriage or waiting for his bill. All that sort of thing he leaves to the opposition firm, whose agents are clamorous for payment, and contrive to accumulate immense sums of the filthy lucre which they affect to despise.

This accommodating fiend is the *bête noir* of the clergy. They are always on his track, or rather he is on theirs. They help us to dodge him, to get out of his way, to be from home when he calls, to escape his meshes, to frustrate his wiles, to save our souls alive-O. "Here you are," they say, "he's coming down the street. We are just running an escape party. If you want to keep out of Hell, come and join us. Don't ask questions. There's no time for that. Hurry up, or you'll be left behind." And when the party turns the corner the clergy say, " Ah, that was a narrow escape. Some of you had a very close shave." And the next morning a collector calls for a subscription for the gentleman who saved you from the Devil.

Nearly fifty thousand gentlemen are engaged in this line of business, to say nothing of the Salvation Army. Ffty thousand Devil Dodgers! And this in England alone. If we include Europe, America, South Africa, and Australia, there are hundreds of thousands of them, maintained at the expense of probably a hundred millions a year. Yet the Devil is not outwitted. Mr. Spurgeon says he is as successful as ever; and, to use Mr. Stead's expression, Spurgeon has " tips from God."

By their own confession, therefore, the Devil Dodgers

are perfectly useless. They take our money, but they do little else. Honesty would make them disband. But they will never do that. They will have to be cashiered, or starved out by cutting off the supplies. The real truth is, they never *were* useful. They were always parasites. They gained their livings by false pretences. They dodged an imaginary enemy. The Devil is played out in educated circles. Presently he will be laughed at by everybody. Then the people will dismiss the priests, and there will be and end of Devil Dodgers.

FIGHTING SPOOKS.

"Spooks" means ghosts, sprites, goblins, and other such phantasms. The word is not yet endenizened in England, but it will probably take out letters of naturalisation here, settle down, and become a very respectable member of the English vocabulary.

Twelve months ago I met an American in London, who told me that he was a Freethinker, but he did not trouble himself about Freethought. His mind was made up on the supernatural, and he did not care to spend his time in "fighting spooks." That is, being emancipated himself from supersitition, he was indifferent about the matter, although millions of his fellow men were still in bondage.

This American gentleman's remark shows how people can be misled by phrases. "Fighting spooks" is a pretty locution, and every Freethinker would admit that fighting spooks is a most unprofitable business. But, in reality, it is not the aggressive Secularist or Atheist who fights these imaginary beings. He fights those who do fight them—which is a very different thing.

Let the priests and preachers of all religions and denominations cease abusing the callow mind of childhood; let them refrain from teaching their fanciful conjectures about "the unseen"; let them desist from peopling the air with the wild creations of their own lawless imagination; let them tell no more than they know, and confine their tongues within the strict limits of honest speech; let them do this, and Freethought will be happy to expire in the blaze of its triumph. There is no joy in fighting superstition, any more than there is joy in attacking disease. Each labor is beneficent and is attended by a *relative* satisfaction; but health is better than the best doctoring, and mental sanity than the subtlest cure.

The clergy are the fighters of spooks. They babble of gods, who get angry with us; of devils, who must be guarded against; of angels, who fly from heaven to earth, and earth to heaven; of saints, who can do us a good turn if they are properly supplicated. But the chief spooks are of course the devils, headed by *the* Devil, Satan, Beelzebub, Lucifer, Abaddon, the Serpent—in short, Old Nick. "We have an army of red coats," said old Fox, "to fight the French; and an army of black coats to fight the Devil—of whom he standeth not in awe."

Before the great procession of Humanity go the priests. "Hush!" they cry, "the hedges are full of devils. Softly, gently, beloved! Do not rush into unspeakable danger. We will bear the brunt of it, out of our fatherly affection for you. See, we stand in front, on the perilous edge of battle. We dare the demons who lie in wait to catch your immortal souls. We beat the bushes, and dislodge them from their hiding-places; strong not in our own strength, but in the grace of God. And behold they fly! Did you not see them? Did you not perceive the flutter of their black wings? Did you not smell their sulphurous taint? Beloved, the road is now clear, the hedges are safe. Forward then! But forget not our loyal services. Remember, beloved, that the laborer is worthy of his hire, and—shell out!"

The services of the black-coats are imaginary, and their payment should be of the same description. Let them live on *their own* faith, and trust to him who fed Elijah in the desert with sandwiches brought by ravens' beaks.

Clearly the belief in spooks is profitable to the clergy. Just as clearly it is expensive to the people. Whistling between the hedges is as good as keeping a parson. But that is not the priest's teaching. He says the spooks are real, and he is the only person to keep them off. Grant the first point, and the second is sure to follow. But *are* the spooks real? Can the clergy show a single live specimen? They cannot, and they know they cannot, either for love or money. Why then does the business hold out? Because an imaginary spook is as good as a real spook, if the clergy can twist and prejudice the youthful mind in their direction. If a showman never lifts the curtain, it does not matter whether he has anything or nothing on the other side.

The belief in spooks is more than profitable to the priests. It enervates and paralyses the human mind. It is the parent of all sorts of mischief. It is our worst inheritance from our savage progenitors. The black spirits that haunted the swamps and forests of primeval ages, and terrified the ape-man who lived in mystery and fear, are not suffered to depart with the ignorance that gave them birth. They are cultivated by priests, and used to overawe the cradles and schools of civilisation.

The Freethinker does not fight spooks. He would not waste an ounce of powder upon them. He fights the fighters of spooks. He assails the superstition on which they flourish. He seeks to free the human mind from gratuitous fears. He dispels the shadows and deepens the sunshine of life.

Surely this is a good work. Whoever takes part in it is giving the race an unmixed blessing. War with the army of enslavement! Down with the seducers of childhood—the spiritual profligates who debauch the youthful mind! Banish them, with their spooks, from the school, the college, the court of justice, the hall of legislation! Let us train generations of sound minds in sound bodies, full of rich blood, and nervous energy, and frank inquiry, and dauntless courage, and starry hope; with faces that never pale at truth, hearts that hold no terms with falsehood, knees that never bend before power or mystery, heads that always keep a manly poise, and eyes that boldly challenge all things from height to depth.

DAMNED SINNERS.

"Thou shalt be brought unto the blood of sprinkling, as an undone helpless, damned sinner."
—JOHN WESLEY, Sermon on "Justification by Faith."

POLITE ears, which are often the longest, will be shocked at the title of this article. This is an age in which it is accounted vulgar to express plain doctrines in plain language. Spurgeon was the last doctor of a good old school. Their theology was hateful: an insult to man and a blasphemy against God—if such a being exists; but they did not beat about the bush, and if they thought you were booked for hell, as was most likely, they took care to let you know it. They called a spade a spade, not a common implement of agricultural industry. They were steeped in Bible English, and did not scruple to use its striking substantives and adjectives. When they pronounced "hell" they aspirated the "h" and gave the full weight of the two "l's." "Damn" and "damnation" shot from their mouths full and round, like a cannon ball sped with a full blast of gunpowder.

But, alas, how are the mighty fallen! No longer do the men of God indulge in thunderous Saxon. They latinise their sermons and diminish the effect of terrible teaching. You shall hear them designate "hell" with twenty roundabout euphemisms, and spin "damnation" into "condemnation" and "damned" into "condemned," until it has not force enough to frighten a cat off a garden wall.

Let us not be blamed, however, if we emulate the plain speech of the honest old theologians, and of the English Bible which is still used in our public schools. We despise the hypocritical cry of "vulgar!" We are going to write, not on "condemned transgressors," but on "damned sinners." Yes, DAMNED SINNERS.

Now, beloved reader, it behoves us to define and distinguish, as well as amplify and expatiate. We must therefore separate the "damned" from the "sinners." Not indeed in fact, for they are inseparable, being in truth one and the same thing; for the adjective is the substantive, and the substantive is the adjective, and the "damned" are "sinners" and "sinners" are the "damned." The separation is merely *mental*, for reasons of *convenience*; just as we separate the inseparable, length from breadth, in our definition of a line. This is necessary to clear and coherent thought; man's mind being finite, and incapable of operating in all directions at once.

What then are *sinners*? A simple question, but not so easy to answer. *All* men are *sinners*. But what is a *man*? A featherless biped? So was the plucked fowl of Diogenes. A man is—well a man; and a sinner is—well a sinner. And this is near enough for most people. But it does not satisfy a rational investigator, to say nothing of your born critic, who will go on splitting hairs till his head is as bare as a plate, and then borrow materials from his neighbor's cranium.

In ancient Egypt it was a sin to kill a cat; in England cats are slain in myriads without a tremor of compunction. Among the Jews it is a sin to eat pork, but an English humorist writes you a delicious essay on Roast Pig. Bigamy is a sin in the whole of Europe but the south-eastern corner, and there it is a virtue, sanctioned by the laws of religion. Marrying your deceased wife's sister is a sin in England; four thousand years ago, in another part of the world, it was no sin at all; in fact, a gentleman of remarkable piety, whom God is said to have loved, married his wife's sister without waiting for a funeral. Did not Jacob take Rachel and Leah together, and walk out with them, one on each arm?

Sin as a *fact* changes with time and place. Sin as an *idea* is disobedience to the law of God; that is, to the doctrines of religion; that is, to the teaching of priests. *Crime* is quite another thing. It is far less heinous, and far more easily forgiven. Of course crime and sin may overlap; they may often be the same thing practically; but this is an accident, for there are crimes that are no sins, and sins that are no crimes. It is a crime, but not a sin, to torture a heretic; it is a sin, but not a crime, to eat meat on a Friday.

A sinner is a person on bad terms with his God. But who, it may be asked, is on good terms with him? No one. According to Christianity, at any rate, we have all sinned; nay, we are all full of original sin; we derived it from our parents, who derived it from Adam, who caught it from Old Nick, who picked it up God knows where.

Now every sinner is a damned sinner. He may not

know it, but he is so; and the great John Wesley advises him to recognise it, and come as a " damned sinner" to God, to be sprinkled or washed with the blood of Christ.

What is *damned* then? We take it that "damned sinners," that is *all* sinners, are persons to whom God says "Damn you!" To whom does he say it? To all sinners; that is, to all men. And why does he say it? Because he is wroth with them. And why is he wroth with them? Because they are sinners. And why are they sinners? Because they are men. And why are they men? Because they cannot help it. They were born in sin and shapen in iniquity, and in sin did their mothers conceive them.

Every Christian admits this — theoretically. He goes to church and confesses himself a "miserable sinner," but if you called him so as he came out of church he would call you something stronger.

A sinner may be damned here, apparently, without being damned hereafter. He is liable to hell until he dies, but after that event he is sometimes reprieved and sent to heaven. But the vast majority of the human race have no share in the atoning blood of Christ. They were " damned sinners" *in posse* before they were born, they are " damned sinners" *in esse* while they live, and they will be " damned sinners " for ever when they leap from this life into eternity, and

> join the immortal fry
> Of almost everybody born to die.

This is a very comfortable doctrine for the narrow, conceited, selfish elect. For other people—all the rest of us—it is calculated to provoke unparliamentary language. Why should God " damn " men? And how can men be "sinners"? Certainly they can sin against each other, because they can injure each other. But how can they sin against God? Can they injure him? He is unchangeable. Can they rob him? He is infinite. Can they deceive him? He is omniscient.

Can they limit his happiness? He is omnipotent. No, they *cannot* sin against him, but he *can* sin against them. And if he exists he *has* sinned against every one of them. Not one human being has ever been as strong, healthy, wise, noble, and happy as God might have made him. Nor is man indebted to God for his creation. There cannot be a debt where there is no contract. It is the creator and not the creature who is responsible, and the theological doctrine of responsibility is the truth turned upside down.

Suppose a man had the power of creating another thinking and feeling being. Suppose he could endow him with any qualities he chose. Suppose he created him sickly, foolish, and vicious. Would he not be responsible for the curse of that being's existence?

Man is what he is because he is. He is practically without choice. The cards are dealt out to him, and he must take them as they come. Is it just to damn him for holding a bad hand? Is it honest to give him hell for not winning the game?

Let us use for a moment the cant language of theology. Let us imagine the *vilest* of "damned sinners" in Gehenna. Does not every scientist, and every philosopher, know that the orb of his fate was predetermined? Would not that "lost soul" have the right to curse his maker? Might he not justly exclaim "I am holier than thou"?

Do not imagine, reader, that this new reading of the book of fate has no practical significance. When we get rid of the idea of "damned sinners," when we abolish the idea of "sin" altogether and its correlative "punishment," and learn to regard man as a complicated effect in a universe of causation, we shall bring wisdom and humanity into our treatment of the "criminal classes," we shall look upon them as moral lunatics and deal with them accordingly. And this spirit will extend itself to all human relations. It will make us less impatient and angry with each other. We shall see that "to know all is to pardon all." Thus will the overthrow of theology be the preparation for a new moral development. Another link of the old serpent of superstition will be uncoiled from the life of humanity, leaving it freer to learn the splendid truth, taught by that divine man Socrates, that wisdom and virtue are one and indivisible.

WHERE IS HELL?

THIS is a question of great importance, or at least of very great interest. According to the Christian scheme of salvation, the vast majority of us will have to spend eternity in "sulphurous and tormenting flames," and we are naturally curious as to the situation of a place in which we shall experience such delightful sensations.

But there is hardly any subject on which we can obtain so little information. The clergy are becoming more and more reticent about it. What little they ever knew is being secreted in the depths of their inner consciousness. When they are pressed for particulars they look injured. Sometimes they piteously exclaim "Don't." At other times they wax wroth, and exclaim to the questioners about the situation of hell, "Wait till you get there."

Just as heaven used to be spoken of as "up above," hell was referred to as "down below." At one time, indeed, it was believed to be underground. Many dark caves were thought to lead to it, and some of them were called "Hell Mouth." Volcanoes were regarded as entrances to the fiery regions, and when

there was an eruption it was thought that hell was
boiling over. Classic mythology, before the time of
Christ, had its entrances to hell at Acherusia, in
Bithynia; at Avernus, in Campania, where Ulysses
began his journey to the grisly abodes; the Sibyl's
cave at Cumæ, in Argolis; at Tænarus, in the southern
Peloponnesus, where Hercules descended, and dragged
Cerberus up to the daylight; and the cave of Trophonius, in Lebadea, not to mention a dozen less noted
places.

The Bible always speaks of hell as "down," and
the Apostles' Creed tells us that Christ "descended"
into hell. Exercising his imagination on this basis,
the learned Faber discovered that after the Second
Advent the saints would dwell on the crust of the
earth, a thousand miles thick, and the damned in a
sea of liquid fire inside. Thus the saints would tread
over the heads of sinners, and flowers would bloom
over the lake of damnation.

Sir John Maundeville, a most engaging old liar,
says he found a descent into hell "in a perilous vale"
in Abyssinia. According to the Celtic legend of
"St. Brandon's Voyage," hell was not "down below,"
but in the moon, where the saint found Judas Iscariot
suffering incredible tortures, but let off every Sunday
to enjoy himself and prepare for a fresh week's agony.
That master of bathos, Martin Tupper, finds this idea
very suitable. He apostrophises the moon as "the
wakeful eye of hell." Bailey, the author of *Festus*, is
somewhat vaguer. Hell, he says, is in a world which
rolls thief-like round the universe, imperceptible to
human eyes:

> a blind world, yet unlit by God,
> Rolling around the extremest edge of light,
> Where all things are disaster and decay.

Imaginations, of course, will differ. While Martin
Tupper and other gentlemen look for hell in the
direction of the moon, the Platonists, according to
Macrobus, reckoned as the infernal regions the whole

space between the moon and the earth. Whiston thought the comet which appeared in his day was hell. An English clergyman, referred to by Alger, maintained that hell was in the sun, whose spots were gatherings of the damned.

The reader may take his choice, and it is a liberal one. He may regard hell as under the earth, or in the moon, or in the sun, or in a comet, or in some concealed body careering through infinite space. And if the choice does not satisfy him, he is perfectly free to set up a theory of his own.

Father Pinamonti is the author of a little book called *Hell Open to Christians*, which is stamped with the authority of the Catholic Church, and issued for the special edification of children. This book declares that hell is four thousand miles distant, but it does not indicate the direction. Anyhow, the distance is so small that the priests might easily set up communication with the place. But perhaps it only exists in the geography or astronomy of faith.

Father Pinamonti seems particularly well informed on this subject. He says the walls of hell are "more than four thousand miles thick." That is a great thickness. But is it quite as thick as the heads of the fools who believe it?

Our belief is that hell is far nearer than the clergy teach. Omar Khayyam, the grand old Persian poet, the "large infidel," as Tennyson calls him, wrote as follows—in the splendid rendering of Edward Fitzgerald:—

> I sent my soul through the invisible,
> Some letter of that after-life to spell,
> And by and bye my soul returned to me,
> And answered, I myself am heaven and hell.

Hell, like heaven, is within us, and about us in the hearts of our fellow-men. Yes, hell is on earth. Man's ignorance, superstition, stupidity, and selfishness, make a hell for him in this life. Let us cease, then, to dread the fabled hell of the priests, and set ourselves to the task of abolishing the real hell of hunger, vice, and misery.

The very Churches are getting ashamed of their theological hell. They are becoming more and more secularised. They call on the disciples of Christ to remedy the evils of this life, and respond to the cry of the poor for a better share of the happiness of this world. Their methods are generally childish, for they overlook the causes of social evil, but it is gratifying to see them drifting from the old moorings, and little by little abandoning the old dogmas. Some of the clergy, like Archdeacon Farrar, go to the length of saying that " hell is not a place." Precisely so, and that is the teaching of Secularism.

SPURGEON AND HELL.

CHARLES LAMB was one of the best men that ever lived. He had his failings, but he never harmed anyone but himself. He was capable of astonishing generosity, and those acquainted with the inner tragedy of his life know that it was a long act of self-denial. He was also extremely modest but not utterly devoid of indignation; and if he could not denounce bitterly, he could speed a shaft of satire into the breast of wickedness or cruelty. On one occasion, in the days of his youth, he was justly annoyed by his friend Coleridge, whose character was very inferior to his own, though he always assumed a tone of moral superiority. Lamb was so

galled by Coleridge's air of virtue and piety, at a
moment when the humorist was suffering terribly in
consequence of his sister's calamity, that he sent the
transcendental poet a list of stinging questions. One
of them asked whether one of the seraphim could
fall, and another whether a man might not be
damned without knowing it.

This last question suggests itself in the case
of Mr. Spurgeon. Mrs. Spurgeon, Dr. Pierson,
and other of the great preacher's friends, are all
assuring us that he is in glory. Writing seven
days after his death, Mrs. Spurgeon said "he has
now been a week in heaven." It is natural
that she should think so, and we do not wish
to rob her of any consolation, nor do we suppose
that this article will ever come under her notice.
But is it not just possible that Spurgeon has
gone to hell? And why should not the question be
raised? We mean no personal offence; we speak in
the interest of justice and truth. Spurgeon was very
glib in preaching about hell, and we do not know
that he had a monopoly of that special line of business. He never blenched at the idea of millions of
human beings writhing in everlasting torment; and
why should it be blasphemy, or even incivility, to
wonder if he himself has gone to perdition?

Predestination, as the Church of England article
says, is wonderfully comforting to the elect; that is,
to those who imagine themselves to be so. But what
if they are mistaken? What if a man, yea a fancied
saint, may be damned without knowing it? God
Almighty has not published lists of the elect. Many
a Calvinistic Pharisee is perhaps a self-elected saint
after all, and at the finish of his journey may find
that he has been walking in the wrong direction.

One of Spurgeon's rooted notions was that
unbelievers were *sure* of hell. They bore the mark
of predestinate damnation broad upon their fore-
heads. Now at the bottom this means that a man

may be damned for believing wrongly. But how can anyone be sure that Spurgeon was absolutely right? The Baptists are only one division of Christians. There are scores of other divisions. All cannot be right, and all may be wrong. Even if one is entirely right, how do we know it is the Baptists? According to the law of probabilities, Spurgeon was very likely in the wrong; and if wrong belief, however sincere, entails damnation, it is quite possible that at 11.5 p.m. on Sunday, January 31, Spurgeon entered Hell instead of Heaven.*

Far be it from us to wish a fellow creature in Hell, but there is always a certain pleasure in seeing the engineer hoist with his own petard. All tragedy has a touch of comedy. Fancy Spurgeon in Hades groaning "I sent other people here by the million, and here I am myself."

How would this be worse than the groan of any other lost soul? Few men are devils or angels. Most are neither black nor white, but grey. Between the best and vilest how much difference is there in the eye of infinite wisdom? And if God, the all-knowing and all-powerful, created men as they are, strong and weak, wise and foolish, good, bad, and indifferent; there is no more injustice in Spurgeon's burning in Hell than in the damnation of the worst wretch that ever cursed the world.

Spurgeon used to preach hell with a certain gusto. Here is a hot and strong passage from his sermon on the Resurrection of the Dead:

"When thou diest, thy soul will be tormented alone; that will be a hell for it; but at the day of judgment thy body will join thy soul, and then thou wilt have twin-hells, thy soul sweating drops of blood, and thy body suffused with agony. In fire exactly like that which we have on earth thy body will lie, asbestos-like, for ever unconsumed, all thy veins roads for the feet of pain to

---

* The next article will explain this matter.

travel on, every nerve a string on which the Devil shall for ever play his diabolical tune of Hell's Unutterable Lament."

After preaching this awful doctrine a man should be ill for a fortnight. Would it not afflict a kind-hearted man unspeakably to think that millions of his fellow beings, or hundreds, or even one, would suffer such a terrible fate? Would it not impair his sleep, and fill his dreams with terror? But it did not have this effect on Spurgeon. After preaching hell in that way, and rolling damnation over his tongue as a dainty morsel, he went home, dined with a good appetite, drank his wine, and smoked his cigar.

There was not the slightest doubt in Spurgeon's mind as to the endless doom of the damned. Here is an extract from another sermon—

"Thou wilt look up there on the throne of God and it shall be written, 'For ever!' When the damned jingle the burning irons of their torment they shall say, 'For ever!' When they howl, echo cries, 'For ever!'

'For ever' is written on their racks,
'For ever' on their chains;
'For ever' burneth in the fire,
'For ever' ever reigns."

How bodies are to burn without consuming, how a fire could last for ever, or how a good God could roast his own children in it, are questions that Spurgeon did not stop to answer. He took the damnable doctrine of damnation as he found it. He knew it was relished by myriads of callous, foolish people; and it gave such a pungent flavor to a long sermon! His listeners were not terrified. Oh dear no! Smith, the Newington greengrocer, was not alarmed; he twirled his thumbs, and said to himself, "Spurgeon's in fine form this morning!"

Archdeacon Farrar protests against the notion of a fiery, everlasting hell as the result of fear, superstition, ignorance, hate, and slavish letter-worship. He declares that he would resign all hope of immortality to save a single human soul from the hell of Mr. Spurgeon. But is not the hell of Mr. Spurgeon the hell of the New Testament? Does not Jesus speak of everlasting fire? Why seek to limit the duration of hell by some hocus-pocus of interpretation? It is idle to pretend that "everlasting" means something less than everlasting. If it means that in relation to hell it must also mean it in relation to heaven. Dr. Farrar cannot have two different meanings for the same word in the same verse; and should he ever go to hell (he will pardon us the supposition), how much consolation would he derive from knowing that his doom was not "everlasting" but only "eternal"? There was more honesty and straightforwardness in Mr. Spurgeon. He preached what the Bible taught him. He set forth a hateful creed in its true colors. His presentation of Christianity will continue to satisfy those who belong to the past, but it will drive many others out of the fold of faith into the broad pastures of Freethought.

IS SPURGEON IN HEAVEN?

WHEN Mrs. Booth died, the wife of the famous "General," the "Army" reported her as "Promoted to Glory from Clacton-on-Sea." It was extremely funny. Clacton-on-Sea is such a prosaic anti-climax after Glory. One was reminded of Sir Horace Glendower Sprat. But the sense of humor is not acute in religious circles.

Mr. Spurgeon frequently gave expression to his dislike and mistrust of the antics of the Salvation Army. He was far from prim himself, but he held that if people were not "won over to Christ" by preaching, it was idle to bait the hook with mere sensationalism. Yet by a strange irony his closest friends, in announcing his death to his flock, actually improved on the extravagance of the Salvationists. Here is a copy of the telegram that was affixed to the rails of the Metropolitan Tabernacle the morning after his decease:

Mentone, 11.50.

Spurgeon's Tabernacle, London.

Our beloved pastor entered heaven 11.5 Sunday night.

HARRALD.

This Harrald was Mr. Spurgeon's private secretary, but he writes like the private secretary of God Almighty. A leading statesman once said he wished he was as cocksure of anything as Tom Macaulay was cocksure of everything; but what was Macaulay's cocksureness to the cocksureness of Harrald? The gentleman could not have spoken with more assurance if he had been Saint Peter himself, and had opened the gate for Pastor Spurgeon.

We take it that Spurgeon expired at 11.5 on Sunday night. That is the *fact*. All the rest is conjecture.

How could his soul enter heaven at the very same moment? Is heaven in the atmosphere? He who asserts it is a very bold speculator. Is it out in the ether? If so, where? And how is it our telescopes cannot detect it? If heaven is a place, as it must be if it exists at all, it cannot very well be within the astronomical universe. Now the farthest stars are inconceivably remote. Our sun is more than 90,000,000 miles distant, and Sirius is more than 200,000 times farther off than the sun. There are stars so distant that their light takes more than a thousand years to reach us, and light travels at the rate of nearly two hundred thousands miles per second!

It is difficult to imagine Spurgeon's soul travelling faster than that; and if heaven is somewhere out in the vast void, beyond the sweep of telescopes or the register of the camera, Spurgeon's soul has so far *not* "entered heaven" that its journey thither is only just begun. In another thousand years, perhaps, it will be nearing the pearly gates. *Perhaps*, we say; for heaven may be a million times further off, and Spurgeon's soul may pull the bell and rouse Saint Peter long after the earth is a frozen ball, and not only the human race but all life has disappeared from its surface. Nay, by the time he arrives, the earth may have gone to pot, and the whole solar system may have vanished from the map of the universe.

What a terrible journey! Is it worth travelling so far to enter the Bible heaven, and sing hymns with the menagerie of the Apocalypse? Besides, a poor soul might lose its way, and dash about the billion-billion-miled universe like a lunatic meteor.

It appears to us, also, that Mr. Harrald and the rest of Mr. Spurgeon's friends have forgotten his own teaching. He thoroughly believed in the bodily resurrection of the dead, and an ultimate day of judgment, when body and soul would join together, and share a common fate for eternity. How is this reconcileable with the notion that Spurgeon's soul "entered heaven at 11.5" on Sunday evening, the thirty-first of January, 1892? Is it credible that the good man went to the New Jerusalem, will stay there in perfect felicity until the day of judgment, and will then have to return to this world, rejoin his old body, and stand his trial at the great assize, with the possibility of having to shift his quarters afterwards? Would not this be extremely unjust, nay dreadfully cruel? And even if Spurgeon, as one of the "elect," only left heaven for form's sake at the day of judgment, to go through the farce of a predetermined trial, would it not be a gratuitous worry to snatch him away from unspeakable bliss to witness the trial of the human species, and the damnation of at least nine-tenths of all that ever breathed?

As a matter of fact, the Christian Church has never been able to make up its mind about the state or position of the soul immediately after death. Only a few weeks ago we saw that Sir G. G. Stokes, unconsciously following in the wake of divines like Archbishop Whately, holds the view that the soul on leaving the body will lie in absolute unconsciousness until the day when it has to wake up and stand in the dock. The controversies on this subject are infinite, and all sorts of ideas have been maintained, but nothing has been authoritatively decided. Mr. Spurgeon's friends have simply *cut* the Gordian knot; that is, they are only dogmatising.

Laying all such subtle disputes aside, we should like Mr. Harrald to tell us how he knows that Spurgeon has gone, is going, or ever will go to heaven. What certainty can they have in the matter? Saint Paul himself alluded to the possibility of his being "a castaway." How can an inferior apostle be *sure* of the kingdom of heaven?

Saint Paul taught predestination, and so did Spurgeon. According to this doctrine, God knew beforehand the exact number of human beings that would live on this planet, though Omniscience itself must have been taxed to decide where the anthropoid exactly shaded off into the man. He also knew the exact number of the elect who would go to heaven, and the exact number of the reprobate who would go to hell. The tally was decided before the spirit of God brooded over the realm of Chaos and old Night. Every child born into the world bears the stamp of his destiny. But the stamp is secret. No one can detect it. Lists of saved and damned are not published. If they were, it would save us a lot of anxiety. Some would say, "I'm all right." Others would say, "I'm in for it; I'll keep cool while I can." But we must all die before we ascertain our fate. We may feel confident of being in the right list, with the rest of the sheep; but confidence is not proof, and impressions are not facts. When we take the great leap we shall know. Until then no man has any certitude; not even the most pious Christian that ever rolled his eyes in prayer to his Maker, or whined out the confession of his contemptible sins. All are in the same perplexity, and Spurgeon was no exception to the rule.

When predestination was really believed, the friends of the greatest saint only *hoped* he had gone to heaven. When they are *sure* of it predestination is dead. Nay, hell itself is extinguished. Spurgeon's friends think he has gone to heaven because they feel he was too good to go to hell. They knew him personally, and it is hard to think that a man whose hand once lay in yours is howling in everlasting fire. Such exceptions prove a new rule. They show that the human heart has outgrown the horrible doctrine of future torment, that the human mind has outgrown foolish creeds, that man is better than his God.

GOD IN JAPAN.

JAPAN has just been visited by a terrible earthquake. Without a moment's warning it swept along, wrecking towns, killing people, and altering the very shape of mountains. A vast tidal wave also rushed against the coast and deluged whole tracts of low-lying country. It is estimated that 50,000 houses have been destroyed, and at least 5,000 men, women, and children. The first reports gave a total of 25,000 slain, but this is said to be an exaggeration. Nevertheless, as a hundred miles or so of railway is torn to pieces, and it is difficult to convey relief to the suffering survivors, the butcher's bill of this catastrophe may be doubled before the finish.

If earthquakes are the work of blind, unconscious Nature, it is idle to spend our breath in discussion or recrimination. Even regret is foolish. We have to take the world as we find it, with all its disadvantages, and make the best of a not too brilliant bargain. Instead of screaming we must study; instead of wailing we must reflect; and eventually, as we gain a deeper knowledge of the secrets of Nature, and a greater mastery over her forces, we shall be better able to foresee the approach of evil and to take precautionary measures against it.

But the standard teaching of England, to say nothing of less civilised nations, is not Naturalism but Theism. We are told that there is a God over all, and that he doeth all things well. On the practical side this deity is called Providence. It is Providence that sends fine weather, and Providence that sends bad weather; Providence that sends floods, and Providence that sends drought; Providence that favors us with a fine harvest, and Providence that blights the crops, reducing millions of people, as in Russia at this moment, to the most desperate shifts of self-preservation. It is Providence that saves Smith's precious life in a railway accident, and of course it is Providence that smashes poor Jones, Brown and Robinson.

Now it will be observed that the favorable or adverse policy of Providence is quite irrespective of human conduct. There is no moral discrimination. If Grace Darling and Jack the Ripper were travelling by the same train, and it met with an accident, everybody knows that their chances of death are precisely equal. If there were any difference it would be in favor of Jack, who seems very careful of his own safety, and would probably take a seat in the least dangerous part of the train.

Some people, of course, and especially parsons, will contend that Providence does discriminate. They have already been heard to hint that the Russian famine is on account of the persecution of the Jews. But this act of brutality is the crime of the Government, and the famine falls upon multitudes of peasants who never saw a Jew in their lives. They have to suffer the pangs of hunger, but the Czar will not go without a single meal or a single bottle of champagne.

No doubt a pious idiot or two will go to the length of asserting or insinuating that the earthquake in Japan is a divine warning to the people, from the Mikado down to his meanest subject, that they are too slow in accepting Christianity. In fact there is a large collection of such pious idiots, only they are deterred by a wholesome fear of ridicule. Hundreds of thousands of people have seen Mr. Wilson Barrett in *Claudian*, without being in the least astonished that an earthquake, which ruins a whole city, should be got up for the hero's spiritual edification.

Let the pious idiots, however numerous, be swept aside, and let the Christian with a fair supply of brains in his skull consider Providence in the light of this earthquake. It is folly to pretend that the Japanese are particularly wicked at this moment. It is greater folly to pretend that the earthquake killed the most flagitious sinners. It slew like Jehovah's bandits in the land of Canaan, without regard to age, sex, or character. The terrible fact must be faced, that in a country not specially wicked, and in a portion of it not inhabited by select sinners, the Lord sent an earthquake to slay man, woman, and child, and if possible to "leave alive nothing that breatheth."

Lay your hand upon your heart, Christian, and honestly answer this question. Would you have done this deed? Of course not. Your cheek flames at the thought. You would rush to save the victims. You would soothe the dying and reverently bury the dead. Why then do you worship a Moloch who laughs at the writhings of his victims and drinks their tears like wine? See, they are working and playing; they are at business and pleasure; one is toiling to support the loved ones at home; another is sitting with them in peace and joy; another is wooing the maiden who is dearer to him than life itself; another is pondering some benevolent project; another is planning a law or a poem that shall be a blessing and a delight to posterity. And lo the mandate of Moloch goes forth, and "his word shall not return unto him void." Swifter than thought calamity falls upon the gay and busy scene. Hearts that throbbed with joy now quiver with agony. The husband folds his wife in a last embrace. The mother gathers her children like Niobe. The lover clasps in the midst of horror the maiden no longer coy. Homes are shaken to dust, halls fall in ruins, the very temples of the gods are shattered. Brains are dashed out, blood flows in streams, limbs are twisted, bodies are pinned by falling masonry, cries of anguish pierce the air, groans follow, and lastly silence. Moloch then retires to his inmost sanctuary, filled and sated with death and pain.

Is it not better, Christian friend, to defy Moloch instead of worshipping him? Is it not still better to regard this deity as the creation of fanciful ignorance? Is not existence a terror if Providence may swoop upon us with inevitable talons and irresistible beak? And does not life become sweeter when we see no cruel intelligence behind the catastrophes of nature?

STANLEY ON PROVIDENCE.

BUCKLE, the historian of Civilisation, points out that superstition is most rampant where men are most oppressed by external nature. Wild and terrible surroundings breed fear and awe in the human mind. Those who lead adventurous lives are subject to the same law. Sailors, for instance, are proverbially superstitious, and military men are scarcely less so. The fighter is not always moral, but he is nearly always religious.

No one acquainted with this truth will be surprised at the piety of explorers. There is a striking exception in Sir Richard Burton, but we do not remember another. From the days of Mungo Park down to our own age, they have been remarkable for their religious temperaments. Had they remained at home, in quiet and safety, they might not have been conspicuous in this respect; but a life of constant adventure, of daily peril and hairbreadth escapes, developed their superstitious tendencies. It is so natural to feel our helplessness in solitude and danger, and perhaps in sickness. It is so easy to feel that our escape from a calamity that hemmed us in on every side was due to a providential hand.

Whether Stanley, who is now the cynosure of all eyes, began with any considerable stock of piety, is a question we have no means of determining; but we can quite understand how a very little would go a very long way in Africa, amid long and painful marches through unknown territory, the haunting peril of strange enemies, and the oppressive gloom of interminable forests. Indeed, if the great explorer had become as superstitious as the natives themselves, we could have forgiven it as a frailty incident to human nature in such trying circumstances. But when he brings his mental weakness home with him, and addresses Englishmen in the language of ideas calculated for the latitude of equatorial Africa, it becomes necessary to utter a protest. Stanley has had a good spell of rest in Egypt, and plenty of time to get rid of the "creeps." He should, therefore, have returned to Europe clothed and in his right mind. But instead of this he deliberately sits down and writes the following rubbish for an American magazine, with one eye on God above and the other on a handsome cheque below:

"Constrained at the darkest hour humbly to confess that without God's help I was helpless, I vowed a vow in the forest solitudes that I would confess his aid before men. Silence, as of death, was round about me; it was midnight; I was weakened by illness, prostrated by fatigue, and wan with anxiety for my white and black companions, whose fate was a mystery. In this physical and mental distress I besought God to give me back my people. Nine hours later we were exulting with a rapturous joy. In full view of all was the crimson flag with the crescent, and beneath its waving folds was the long-lost rear column."

Danger and grief are apt to make us selfish, and no one would be hard on Stanley for showing weakness in such circumstances. But he rather glories in it. The danger is gone, and alas! the egotism remains. Others perished miserably, but he escaped. Omnipotence took care of him and let them go to the Devil. No doubt they prayed in their extremity as heartily as he did, but their prayers were unheard or neglected. Stanley was the lion of the party. Yes, and in parading his egotistic piety in this way, he is in danger of becoming a *lion comique*.

There is something absolutely farcical in Stanley's logic. While he was praying to God, millions of other persons were engaged in the same occupation. Agonised mothers were beseeching God to spare their dear children; wives were imploring him to restore the bread-winner of the family to health; entombed miners were praying in the dark depths of coalpits, and slowly perishing of starvation; shipwrecked sailors were asking for the help that never came. Providence could not, apparently, take on too much business at once, and while Stanley's fate trembled in the balance the rest of mankind might shift for themselves.

But the farce does not end here. Stanley's attitude was much like Jacob's. That smooth-skinned and smooth-tongued patriarch said that if God would guarantee him a safe journey, feed him, clothe him, find him pocket money, and bring him safe back again—well, then the Lord should be his God. Stanley was not so exacting, but his attitude was similar. He asked God to give him back his people (a few short, killed or starved, did not matter), and promised in return to "confess his aid before men." Give me the solid pudding, he says, and I will give you the empty praise. And now he is safe back in Europe he fulfils his part of the contract, and goes about trumpeting the praise of Omnipotence; taking care, however, to get as much cash as possible for every note he blows on the instrument.

Even this does not end the farce. Stanley's piety runs away with his arithmetic. He reminds us of a Christian lady we heard of the other day. She prayed one night, on going to bed, for news from her daughter, and early the next morning a letter came bearing the Edinburgh post-mark. This was clearly an answer to her prayer. But a sceptical friend showed her that the letter must have been posted at Edinburgh before she prayed for it. Now Stanley reasons like that lady. Nine hours is no time in central Africa. The "long-lost rear column" must have been near, though invisible, when Stanley struck his little bargain with the Almighty. Had it been two or three hundred miles off, and miraculously transported, the hand of Providence would have been unmistakable; but in the circumstances its arrival was natural, and the miracle is obviously the creation of Stanley's heated brain. He was "weakened by illness" and "prostrated by fatigue," and the absurdity was pardonable. We only protest against his playing the child when he is well and strong.

GONE TO GOD.

STANLEY, the African traveller, is a man of piety. He seems to be on pretty familiar terms with the "one above." During his last expedition to relieve Emin— a sceptical gentleman, who gets along with less bloodshed than Stanley—he was troubled with "traitors"; that is, black fellows who thought they had a better right in Africa than the intrusive whites, and acted upon that opinion. This put Stanley in a towering rage. He resolved to teach the "traitors" a lesson. One of them was solemnly tried—by his executioners, and sentenced to be hung. A rope was noosed round his neck, and he was taken under a tree, which was to be his gallows. The poor devil screamed for mercy, but Stanley bent his inexorable brows, and cried, "Send him to God!"

"We were troubled with no more traitors," says Stanley. Very likely. But the great man forgot to say what he meant by the exclamation, "Send him to God!" Did he mean "Send him to God for judgment?" If so, it was rather rough to hang the prisoner before his proper trial. Did he mean, "The fellow isn't fit for earth, so send him to heaven?" If so, it was a poor compliment to Paradise. Or did he simply use a pious, impressive form of speech to awe the spectators, and give them the notion that he had as much traffic with God as any African mystery-man or Mohammedan dervish?

The middle one of these three theories fits in best with the general sentiment, or at any rate the working sentiment, of Christian England. Some brutal, drunken, or passionate wretch commits a murder. He is carefully tried, solemnly sentenced, and religiously hanged. He is declared unfit to live on this planet. But he is still a likely candidate for heaven, which apparently yawns to receive all the refuse of earth. He is sedulously taken in hand by the gaol chaplain, or some other spiritual guide to glory, and is generally brought to a better frame of mind. Finally, he expresses sorrow for his position, forgives everybody he has ever injured, delivers himself of a good deal of highly edifying advice, and then swings from the gallows clean into the Kingdom of Heaven.

The grotesque absurdity of all this is enough to wrinkle the face of a cab horse. Society and the murderer are both playing the hypocrite, and of course Society is the worse of the two, for it is acting deliberately and methodically, while the poor devil about to be hung is like a hunted thing in a corner, up to any shift to ease his last moments and make peace with the powers of the life to come. Society says he has killed somebody, and he shall be killed; that he is not fit to live, but fit to die; that it must strangle him, and call him "brother" when the white cap is over his face, and God must save his soul; that he is too bad to dwell on earth, but it hopes to meet him in heaven.

Religion does not generate sense, logic, or humaneness in the mind of Society. Its effect on the doomed assassin is simply horrible. He is really a more satisfactory figure when committing the murder than when he is posing, and shuffling and twisting, and talking piously, and exhibiting the intense, unmitigated selfishness which is at the bottom of all religious sentiment. The essence of piety comes out in this tragi-comedy. Personal fear, personal hope, self, self, self, is the be-all and the end-all of this sorry exhibition.

A case in point has just occurred at Leeds. James Stockwell was hung there on Tuesday morning. While under sentence of death, the report says, he slept well and ate heartily, so that remorse does not appear to have injured his digestion or any other part of his physical apparatus. On learning that he would not be reprieved, and must die, he became very attentive to the chaplain's ministrations; in fact, he took to preaching himself, and wrote several letters to his relatives, giving them sound teetotal advice, and warning them against the evils of drink.

But the fellow lied all the time. His crime was particularly atrocious. He outraged a poor servant girl, sixteen years of age, and then cut her throat. He was himself thirty-two years of age, with a wife and one child, so that he had not even the miserable excuse of an unmated animal. A plea of insanity was put forward on his behalf, but it did not avail. When the wretched creature found he was not to be reprieved, and took kindly to the chaplain's religion, he started a fresh theory to cover his crime. He said he was drunk when he committed it. Now this was a lie. The porter's speech in *Macbeth* will explain our meaning. James Stockwell may have had a glass, but if he was really drunk, in the sense of not knowing what he was about, we believe it was simply impossible for him to make outrage the prelude to murder. If he had merely drunk enough to bring out the beast in him, without deranging the motor nerves, he was certainly not *drunk* in the proper sense of the word. He knew what he was doing, and both in the crime and in his flight he showed himself a perfect master of his actions.

Religion, therefore, did not " convict him of sin." It did not lay bare before him his awful wickedness. It simply made him hypocritical. It induced or permitted him to save his *amour propre* by a fresh falsehood.

James Stockwell's last letter from gaol was written the day before his execution. It was a comprehensive epistle, addressed to his father and mother and brothers and sisters. "God" and "Christ" appear in it like an eruption. The writer quotes the soothing text, "Come unto me all you that labor and are heavy laden and I will give you rest." He was evidently familiar with Scripture, and thought this text especially applicable to himself. "Many a prayer," he says, "have I offered to God both on behalf of you and myself," and he winds up by "hoping to meet you all hereafter."

Not a word about his crime. Not a word about his injury to society. Not a word about the poor girl he outraged and murdered. James Stockwell had no thought for her or her relatives. He did not trouble about what had become of Kate Dennis. He was careless whether she was in heaven or hell. Not once, apparently, did it cross his mind that he had destroyed her young life after nameless horror; that he had killed her in the bloom of maidenhood; that at one fell swoop he had extinguished all that she might have been—perhaps a happy wife and mother, living to a white old age, with the prattle of grandchildren soothing her last steps to the grave. Such reflections do not occur to gentlemen who are anxious about their salvation, and in a hurry to get to heaven.

"I and mine"—my fate, my mother, my father, my sisters, my brothers—this was the sole concern of James Stockwell under the chaplain's ministrations. In this frame of mind, we presume, he has sailed to glory, and his family hope to meet him there snug in Abraham's bosom. Well, we don't. We hope to give the haunt of James Stockwell a wide berth. If he and others like him are in the upper circles, every decent person would rather be in the pit.

Let not the reader suppose that James Stockwell's case is uncommon. We have made a point of reading the letters of condemned murderers, and they all bear a family likeness. Religion simply stimulates and sanctifies selfishness. In selfishness it began and in selfishness it ends. Extreme cases only show the principle in a glaring light; they do not alter it, and the light is the light of truth.

James Stockwell has gone to God. No doubt the chaplain of Leeds gaol feels sure of it. Probably the fellow's relatives are just as sure. But what of Kate Dennis. Is *she* with God? What an awful farce it would be if she were in hell. Perhaps she is. She had no time to prepare for death. She was cut off "in her sins." But her murderer had three weeks to prepare for his freehold in New Jerusalem. He qualified himself for a place with the sore-legged Lazarus. He dwells in the presence of the Lamb. He drinks of the river of life. He twangs his hallelujah harp and blows his hallelujah trumpet. Maybe he looks over the battlements and sees Kate Dennis in Hades. The murderer in heaven, and the victim in hell! Nay more. It has been held that the bliss of the saved will be heightened by witnessing the tortures of the damned. In that case Kate Dennis may burn to make James Stockwell's holiday. He will watch her writhings with more than the relish of a sportsman who has hooked a lusty trout. "Ha, ha," the worthy James may exclaim, "I tortured her before I killed her, and now I shall enjoy her tortures for ever."

THANK GOD.

THE peculiarly selfish character of religion is often exemplified, but we do not remember a better illustration than the one which recently occurred at Folkestone. The twenty-seven seamen who were rescued from the *Benvenue* attended a thanksgiving service at the parish church, where the vicar delivered " a short address suitable to the occasion." Their captain and four of his crew were drowned, and the lucky survivors thanked the Lord for saving them, though he let the others perish in the yeasty waves.

We should like to see a copy of that vicar's suitable discourse. We suspect it would be an interesting study to a cynic. No doubt the man of God's chief motive was professional. The saving of those shipwrecked men was a splendid piece of work, but it required to be rounded off. It was not complete unless the parson blessed it and approved it with a text. He came in at the finish when the danger was all over, and gave the perfecting touch in the shape of a cheap benediction.

Probably the man of God put in a good word for Providence. The poor sailors had been snatched from the jaws of death; their minds were therefore in a state of agitation, and at the very best they are not a logical or reflective race of men. Very likely, therefore, they assented to the theory that they owed their deliverance to the blessing of God, but a little quiet thought about the matter would possibly make them see it in a different light.

The persons who visibly *did* save them from drowning were gallant lifeboat-men, who put their own lives in deadly peril, fighting the storm inch by inch in the hope of rescuing a number of unknown fellow creatures. All honor to *them!* We would sooner doff the hat to them than to any prince in Christendom. Some of them, perhaps, take a drop too much occasionally, and their language may often be more vigorous than polite. But all that is superficial. The real test of a man is what he will do when he is put to it. When those rough fellows saw a brave task before them, all the skin-deep blackguardism dropped away; the heroic came out in supreme majesty, and they were consecrated by it more truly than any smug priest at his profitable altar. As they jumped into the boat they proved the nobility of human nature, and the damnable falsehood of the Christian doctrine of original sin.

What share Providence had in the matter is not very apparent. Strong arms and stout hearts were in the lifeboat, and that accounts for her reaching the wreck. Had the rowers the choice of a stimulus, we dare say they would have taken a swig of brandy in preference to any quantity of the Holy Spirit. What Providence *might* have done if he, she, or it was in the humor, was to keep the shipwrecked sailors safe until the lifeboat arrived. But this was *not* done. Those who were lashed to the rigging were saved, while the captain and four others, less fortunately situated, were lost. Where the *material* means were efficacious there was salvation, and where they failed there was disaster and death.

So much for the logical side of the matter. Now let us look at the moral side. Religion pretends to minister to the unselfish part of our nature. That is the theory, but how does it work out in practice? Thanking God for saving the survivors of a shipwreck implies that he could have saved those who perished. It also implies that he did not choose to do so. It further implies that the saved are more worthy, or more important, than the lost; at least, it implies that they are greater favorites in the "eye of heaven." Now this is a frightful piece of egotism, which everyone with a spark of manhood would be disgusted at if he saw it in its true colors.

Nor is this all. It is not even the worst. There is a viler aspect of this "thanksgiving" business. One man is saved in a disaster and another is killed. When the first realises his good luck he congratulates himself. This is natural and pardonable, but only for a moment. The least disinterestedness, the least sympathy, the least imagination, would make him think of his dead companion. "Did he suffer much, poor fellow? What will his wife do? How will his little ones get on without a father? After all, mightn't it have been better if he had been spared instead of me? Who knows?"

If these reflections did not occur under the stimulated instinct of self-preservation it would be bad enough. How much worse when the survivor keeps up the selfish attitude in cold blood, and deliberately goes about thanking God for *his* preservation! Ordinary reason and humanity would cry shame on such egotism, but religion steps in and sanctifies it.

Some of these days an honest man will be provoked into a bit of good strong "blasphemy." When he hears a fellow thanking Providence for *his* safety, while others perished, this honest man will shrug his shoulders. And when the fellow cries "Bless God!" this honest man will exclaim "Damn God!"

No doubt the priests would burn that honest man alive if they had the power. But his logic and his feelings will be better than theirs. He will abhor selfishness even in the disguise of piety, and he will argue that if God is to be credited with the lives of those who are saved, he should also be debited with the lives of those who are lost. And how would the account stand then?

JUDGMENT DAY.

The end of the world has been a fertile and profitable theme with pulpit mountebanks and pious adventurers. Ever since the primitive ages of Christianity it has served to frighten the credulous and feather the nests of their deceivers.

In the apostolic days the Second Coming of Christ

was generally and constantly expected. According to the twenty-fourth of Matthew, Jesus predicted that the end of all things would soon arrive. The sun and moon were to be darkened; the stars were to fall from heaven; and the Son of Man was to come through the clouds with great power and glory, and gather the elect together from every quarter of the earth. According to the twenty-fifth of Matthew, this wondrous scene was to be followed by a Great Assize. All the nations were to be judged before the heavenly throne, and divided into two lots, one destined for heaven and the other for hell. And Jesus significantly added, " Verily I say unto you, this generation shall not pass, till all these things be fulfilled."

St. Paul also, in the fourth chapter of the first of Thessalonians, said that the Lord would " descend from heaven with a shout, with the voice of the archangel, and with the trump of God: and the dead in Christ shall rise first: Then we which are alive and remain shall be caught up together with them in the clouds, to meet the Lord in the air."

Nothing of the sort has happened. There is no sign of the Lord's coming, and he is already eighteen centuries behind date. " Behold I come quickly"— " Surely I come quickly." Such was the announcement. But, like many other divine promises, it has been falsified. The only orthodox way out of the difficulty is to say that the Lord does not reckon time as we do; with him a day is as a thousand years, and a thousand years as a day.

The general public, however, eighteen hundred years ago, did not know how long the prophecy was to remain unfulfilled, and it had an extraordinary power over them. Being mostly very ignorant, and therefore very credulous, they were easily terrified by the notion that the world was to be burnt up speedily; and they as readily embraced the doctrine which promised to bring them safely through the catastrophe. From the way in which the game answers still with the Christian mob, after nearly two thousand years of exposure, we can understand what a splendid instrument of proselytising it must have been in the hands of the fanatical preachers of the early Church. Combine with it the Millennium promised to the saints after the Second Coming of Christ, in which they were to enjoy themselves royally, and you will feel the justice of Gibbon's remark that "it must have contributed in a very considerable degree to the progress of the Christian faith." It was inculcated by a succession of Fathers, from Justin Martyr to Lactantius. But when it had served its purpose it was allowed to drop. As Gibbon says, "it was at first treated as a profound allegory, was considered by degrees as a doubtful and useless opinion, and was at length rejected as the absurd invention of heresy and fanaticism." The Millennium is stigmatised, in what once stood as the forty-first Article of the English Church, as "a fable of Jewish dotage." We wonder whether the plain-spoken divines who drew drew up that article included Jesus Christ, St. Paul, and St. John among the Jewish dotards.

At the end of the tenth century the doctrine of the Second Coming was revived. The people were led to believe that the old serpent's thousand years of bondage was nearly up, that he would be let loose about the year 1,000, that Antichrist would then appear, and that the end of the world would follow. Churches and houses were therefore left to decay, as they would cease to be wanted. Whenever an eclipse of the sun or moon took place, the people ran into caverns and caves. Multitudes hurried off to Palestine, where they supposed Christ would make his descent. They transferred their property to the priests, who could say with Iago, "thus do I ever make my fool my purse." Others not only gave their property to the priests, but actually became their slaves; hoping, says Mosheim, that "the supreme Judge would be more favorable to them if they made themselves servants to *his* servants."

Jortin justly observes that the priests industriously cherished the delusion for the sake of filthy lucre. They accepted the gifts of their poor dupes, although earthly possessions would be as useless to them as to the laity if the last days were at hand. Donations to the Church were given by fools and received by knaves. The reason assigned for the gift is generally thus expressed : *Appropinquante mundi termino—The end of the world being now at hand.*

When the tenth century ended without a sign of the Second Advent, people looked at each other and said " He is not come then." And the priests chuckled, "No, he has not come, but your property is gone." There was no chance of bringing an action for obtaining money under false pretences, and Holy Mother Church never gives back a farthing of what she obtains, for what is once devoted to God can never be alienated without sacrilege.

Although the delusion has been milder since then, it has always lurked among the ignorant, and occasionally become acute. Silly Christians still shake their heads when a comet is visible, and regard it as a blazing portent. They even hint that one of these wanderers through space may collide with our globe and cause the final smash; not knowing that comets are quite harmless, and that hundreds of cubic miles of their tails would not outweigh a jar-ful of air.

Dr. Cumming foretold the grand collapse several times. His books were read by thousands of superstitious people. Finally, he was played out, and he went to his grave a discredited prophet. Had he been wiser he would have fixed the event some time after he was likely to be buried. Then the game would have lasted his lifetime, and what does it matter if you are found out when you are dead?

How far Cumming believed his own prophecies is a moot point. It is said that he bought the lease of a house, which expired about twenty-five years after his date for the day of judgment.

Prophet Baxter, of the *Christian Herald*, now runs the business. He wrote a book to prove that Louis Napoleon was Antichrist. Louis Napoleon is dead and nearly forgotten. Then he proved that Gambetta was Antichrist. Gambetta is dead and not forgotten. Then he proved that Prince Jerome was Antichrist. Prince Jerome is nowhere, and Baxter is looking out for a fresh Antichrist. Yet his paper is read by hundreds of thousands. As Heine said, the fool-crop is perennial.

Over in America the Second Adventists are a numerous body. They watch and pray for the coming of Christ, and keep white robes ready for their ascension. Some time ago they donned their linen in the expectation that the Lord was coming that very night. But the Lord did not put in an appearance, and the robes were laid up in lavender again. A fat matron trying to fly in that outfit would be a sight worth seeing. It would take several angels to float some of them. Even the archangel Michael might shrink from tackling twenty-stone.

Like everything else in Christianity, except the accursed doctrine of salvation by faith, the idea of the end of the world and a day of judgment is derived from older sources.

The Hindu *Kalpas*, covering thousands of millions of years, are periods of creation and destruction, and each is called a day of Brahma. During this enormous interval the universe begins and ends. Brahma wakes from his slumbrous solitude, and his thoughts and emotions embody themselves in worlds and creatures. When he falls to rest again, the whole system of finite things vanishes like the baseless fabric of a vision.

The Stoics also believed in a periodical destruction and renovation of all things. They, as Alger says, "conceived of God as a pure artistic force or seed of universal energy, which exhibits its history in the evolution of the cosmos, and, on its completion, blossoms into fire and vanishes. The universal periodical conflagration destroys all evil, and leaves the indestructible God alone in his pure essence again."

The Persians entertained a similar conception, which more closely resembles the Christian doctrine. Ahura-Mazda creates all things good, and the race of men happy and immortal. But Angra-Mainyas, his adversary, the old serpent, corrupts them, brings upon them misery and death, and leads their souls to his dark abode. Good and evil spirits fill all creation with their conflict. But at last Ahura-Mazda subdues Angra-Mainyas, nullifies all the mischief he has done by means of a great deliverer, who is sent to instruct and redeem mankind, raises the dead, purifies the world with fire, and restores all nature to its paradisiacal condition.

The Scandinavians had their Ragnarök, or Twilight of the Gods, when all the powers of good and evil join in battle. The horn sounds, the last day dawns in fire and splendor from the sky, in fog and venom from the abyss. Flames destroy the earth, the combatants mostly slay each other, but Gimli, the heaven of the All-Father, is a refuge for the survivors, and the beginning of a new and fairer world.

Chiefly influenced by the Persian, and partly by other systems, the later Jewish theology, as represented by the Pharisees, taught that Jehovah would reappear in the last days; and the Day of the Lord, which in former ages meant any national calamity, became transformed into the Day of Judgment. What was to happen on that occasion is described in the Book of Enoch. This was written about a century before Christ, yet it is quoted in the Epistle of Jude as the work of old transported Enoch, the seventh from Adam; a fact which throws a singular light on the critical acumen of the early Christians. Jesus Christ, Paul, and especially the author of Revelation, are indebted to the Book of Enoch. It provided them with nearly all the plot, dialogue and scenery of their judgment drama.

As judges of the dead, the Greeks had Minos, who presided at the trial of souls from Europe; Rhadamanthus, who examined those from Asia; and Æacus, who tried those from Africa. America and Australia were then unknown, and souls from those continents were not provided with inspectors. Of course the dead who held communication with the living, never told them more than they knew. The same thing continues to this day. All the messages from the departed given at all the Spiritist *séances* have not added a single fragment to the world's stock of information.

The ancient Egyptians believed in "after death the judgment." Souls were tried in the Hall of the two Truths, or the double Justice. They were weighed in the balance. Thoth noted the result, and Osiris pronounced sentence. Before burial, also, the Egyptian dead underwent a saner trial. The friends and relatives, the enemies and accusers of the deceased, assembled around the sarcophagus before forty-two assessors. He was put on his trial before them; and if justified, awarded an honorable burial; but, if condemned, disgraced by the withholding of funeral rites. Kings, as well as commoners, were apparently subject to the same ordeal. Does this account for the beneficent character of their government, and the prosperous content of the people, which is reflected in the placid smile of their sphinxes?

Probably the antique notion of a general Day of Judgment arose from the imposing trials, where the King sat in judgment, throned, jewelled, and guarded; where all were free to approach and claim justice; and where the sentences were executed by the soldiers directly they were passed. Add to this scene a general *auto da fé*, in which Christ plays the part of Grand Inquisitor, the saints that of familiars, and the Devil that of executioner, and you have a very fair idea of the Christian Day of Judgment.

" Day," we presume, must not be taken too literally. The Mohammedans believe the Great Assize will last

thousands of years. In that case the people who are
fond of hearing trials will have a fine time, until their
own turn comes. After all, even the Mohammedan
computation seems too slender. To say nothing of the
scientific antiquity of man, and reckoning according to
the Bible chronology, about two hundred thousand
million souls have passed into eternity already, and the
Lord knows how many more will join them. Imagination fails in conceiving the time it would take to try
all that multitude, especially if there are a good number
of Tichborne cases. Besides, the whole thing seems
unfair. Those who get a ticket for heaven at the end
of the Day will enjoy a few thousand years less of bliss
than the more fortunate ones who came early; and
those who get a ticket for hell in the first hour will
suffer a few thousand years of torture more than those
who are sentenced at the finish.

The criterion at the Day of Judgment will be Faith.
That is a difficult virtue to wise men, and an easy one
to fools. The ninnies, therefore, will have the best
chance. This must be very consoling to mankind if
Carlyle's estimate of England's population—"thirty
millions, mostly fools"—may be extended to the rest
of the world.

All who have faith enough to secure a seat in heaven
are called "sheep," and they could not be labelled
better. All the others are called "goats," that is,
lusty, strong-legged fellows who despise the game of
follow-my-leader, who object to walking along the road
made for them, and are always leaping the fence to see
what is on the other side. There was war in heaven
once, we are told, but that was before Satan and his
crew were kicked out. There will never be war in
heaven again. Jesus Christ will easily be able to
manage his sheep. But the Devil will have a tougher
job with his goats. There will always be a kingdom in
heaven, but ten to one there will be a republic in hell.

Christianity says we are to be saved by faith. Our
view is different. Men are saved by thinking and

acting. While Christian monks were trying to degrade men below the level of brutes, some unknown Secularists invented windmills and glass windows. While the Inquisition was exterminating heresy and purifying the faith, Galileo was inventing the telescope. While Church of Englandism and Methodism were fighting over the faith in England, Watt was discovering the use of steam. Faith never saved men here, and why should it save them hereafter? God, if he exist, must be too humane and sensible to judge men according to their belief; and if he endowed us with reason, he will never damn us for exercising it.

Wandering in an immense forest during the night, said Diderot, I have only one little light to guide me. A stranger comes to me and says, "My friend, blow out your candle to find your way better." That light is reason, and that stranger is a theologian.

Science, no less than common sense, dispels Christian superstition. Evolution destroys the idea of a general catastrophe. There was a time when life could not exist on the earth, and there will probably come a time when it will cease to exist. Long before then man will have disappeared. But the æon of our race may extend to millions of years. Is not this time practically infinite? And do not those who make it a cause for lamentation and despair resemble the man that Spinoza ridicules, who refuses to eat his dinner to-day because he is not sure of a dinner for ever and ever? Sit down, you fool, and eat.

SHELLEY'S ATHEISM.*

CHARLES DARWIN, the Newton of biology, was an Agnostic—which is only a respectable synonym for an Atheist. The more he looked for God the less he could find him. Yet the corpse of this great "infidel" lies in Westminster Abbey. We need not wonder, therefore, that Christians and even parsons are on the Shelley Centenary committee, or that Mr. Edmund Gosse was chosen to officiate as high pontiff at the Horsham celebration. Mr. Gosse is a young man with a promising past—to borrow a witticism from Heine. In the old *Examiner* days he hung about the army of revolt. Since then he has become a bit of a Philistine, though he still affects a superior air, and retains a pretty way of turning a sentence. The selection of such a man to pronounce the eulogy on Shelley was in keeping with the whole proceedings at Horsham, where everybody was lauding a "bogus Shelley," as Mr. Shaw remarked at the Hall of Science celebration.

Mr. Gosse was good enough to tell the Horsham celebrants that "it was not the poet who was attacked" in Shelley's case, but "the revolutionist, the enemy of kings and priests, the extravagant and paradoxical humanitarian." Mr. Gosse generously called this an "intelligent aversion," and in another sense than his it undoubtedly was so. The classes, interests, and abuses that were threatened by Shelley's principles, acted with

---

* On August 4, 1892, the centenary of Shelley's birth was celebrated at Horsham, where it is intended to found a Shelley Library, if not a Shelley Museum. The celebrants were a motley collection. They were all concealing the poet's principles and paying honor to a bogus Shelley. A more honest celebration took place in the evening at the Hall of Science, Old-street, London, E.C. Six or seven hundred people were addressed by Dr. Furnivall, G. B. Shaw, and G. W. Foote; and every pointed reference to Shelley's religious, social, and political heresy was enthusiastically applauded.

the intelligence of self-preservation. They gave him an ill name and would gladly have hung him. Yes, it was, beyond all doubt, an "intelligent aversion." Byron only dallied with the false and foolish beliefs of his age, but Shelley meant mischief. This accounts for the hatred shown towards him by orthodoxy and privilege.

Mr. Gosse himself appears to have an "intelligent aversion" to Shelley's *principles*. He professes a great admiration for Shelley's *poetry*; but he regards it as a sort of beautiful landscape, which has no other purpose than gratifying the æsthetic taste of the spectator. For the poet's *teaching* he feels or affects a lofty contempt. Shelley the singer was a marvel of delicacy and power; but Shelley the thinker was at best a callow enthusiast. Had he lived as long as Mr. Gosse, and moved in the same dignified society, he would have acquired an "intelligent aversion" to the indiscretions of his youthful passion for reforming the world; but fate decided otherwise, and he is unfortunate enough to be the subject of Mr. Gosse's admonitions.

Shelley lived like a Spartan; a hunk of bread and a jug of water, dashed perhaps with milk, served him as a dinner. His income was spent on the poor, on struggling men of genius, and on necessitous friends. Now as the world goes, this is simply asinine; and Mr. Gosse plays to the Philistine gallery by sneering at Shelley's vegetarianism, and playfully describing him as an "eater of buns and raisins." It was also lamented by Mr. Gosse that Shelley, as a "hater of kings," had an attraction for "revolutionists," a set of persons with whom Mr. Gosse would have no sort of dealings except through the policeman. "Social anarchists," likewise, gathered "around the husband of Godwin's daughter"—a pregnant denunciation, though it leaves us in doubt whether Shelley, Godwin, or Mary was the anarch, or all three of them together; while the "husband" seems to imply that getting married was one of the gravest of Shelley's offences.

But the worst of all is to come: "Those to whom the restraints of religion were hateful marshalled themselves under the banner of the youth who had rashly styled himself as an Atheist, forgetful of the fact that all his best writings attest that, whatever name he might call himself, he, more than any other poet of the age, saw God in everything."

We beg to tell Mr. Gosse that he is libellous and impertinent. He knows little or nothing of Atheists if he thinks they are only repelled by the "restraints of religion." They have restraints of their own, quite as numerous and imperative as those of any religionist who fears his God. What is more, they have incentives which religion weakens. Mr. Gosse is perhaps in a state of ignorance on this matter. He probably speaks of the moral condition of Atheists as a famous American humorist proposed to lecture on science, with an imagination untrammeled by the least acquaintance with the subject.

So much (it is quite enough) for the libel; and now for the impertinence. Mr. Gosse pretends to know Shelley's mind better than he knew it himself. Shelley called himself an Atheist; that is indisputable; but he did so "rashly." He was mistaken about his own opinions; he knew a great many things, but he was ignorant of himself. But the omniscient Mr. Gosse was born (or *was* he *born?*) to rectify the poet's blunder, and assure the world that he was a Theist without knowing it—in fact, a really God-intoxicated person.

What wonder is it that Mr. Gosse became intoxicated in turn, and soared in a rapture of panegyric over a Shelley of his own construction? "The period of prejudice is over," he exclaimed, "and we are gathered here to-day under the auspices of the greatest poet our language has produced since Shelley died, encouraged by universal public opinion and by dignitaries of all the professions—yea, even by prelates of our national Church." Here the preacher's intoxication became maudlin, and there should have been an interval for soda-water.

Curiously enough, the very last page of Trelawny's *Records of Shelley and Byron* contains a conversation between that gallant friend of the two poets and a " prelate of our national Church."

"Some years ago, one of the most learned of the English Bishops questioned me regarding Shelley; he expressed both admiration and astonishment at his learning and writings. I said to the Bishop, 'You know he was an Atheist.' He said, 'Yes.' I answered: 'It is the key and the distinguishing quality of all he wrote. Now that people are beginning to distinguish men by their works, and not creeds, the critics, to bring him into vogue, are trying to make out that Shelley was not an Atheist, that he was rather a religious man. Would it be right in me, or anyone who knew him, to aid or sanction such a fraud?' The Bishop said: 'Certainly not, there is nothing righteous but truth.' And there our conversation ended."

Trelawny's bishop was willing (outside church, and in private conversation) to deprecate prejudice and acknowledge the supremacy of truth; and perhaps for that reason he allowed that Shelley *was* an Atheist. Mr. Gosse's bishops will soon be converting him into a pillar of the Church.

Trelawny knew Shelley a great deal better than Mr. Gosse. He enjoyed an intimate friendship with the poet, not in his callow days, but during the last year or two of his life, when his intellect was mature, and his genius was pouring forth the great works that secure his immortality. During that time Shelley professed the opinions he enunciated in *Queen Mab*. He said that the matter of that poem was good; it was only the treatment that was immature. Again and again he told Trelawny that he was content to know nothing of the origin of the universe; that religion was chiefly a means of deceiving and robbing the people; that it fomented hatred, malice, and all uncharitableness; and that it also fettered the intellect, deterring men from solving the problems of individual and social life, as well as the problems of nature, out of regard for the supposed oracles of Omniscience, which were after all the teachings of bigoted and designing priests. Shelley called himself an Atheist; he wrote "Atheist" after his name on a famous occasion; and Trelawny says "he never regretted having done this."

"The principal fault I have to find," wrote Trelawny, "is that the Shelleyan writers, being Christians themselves, seem to think that a man of genius cannot be an Atheist, and so they strain their own faculties to disprove what Shelley asserted from the earliest stage of his career to the last day of his life. He ignored all religions as superstitions."

On another occasion Shelley said to Trelawny—"The knaves are the cleverest; they profess to know everything; the fools believe them, and so they govern the world." Which is a most sagacious observation. He said that "Atheist!" in the mouth of orthodoxy was "a word of abuse to stop discussion, a painted devil to frighten the foolish, a threat to intimidate the wise and good."

Mr. Gosse may reply that Shelley's conversations with Trelawny are not absolute evidence; that they were written down long afterwards, and that we cannot be sure of Shelley's using the precise words attributed to him. Very well then; be it so. Mr. Gosse has appealed to Shelley's "writings," and to Shelley's writings we will go. True, the epithet "best" is inserted by Mr. Gosse as a saving qualification; but we shall disregard it, partly because "best" is a disputable adjective, but more because *all* Shelley's writings attest his Atheism.

Let us first go to Shelley's prose, not because it is his "best" work (though some parts of it are exquisitely beautiful, often very powerful, and always chaste), but because prose is less open than verse to false conception and interpretation. In the fine fragment "On Life" he acutely observes that "Mind, as far as we have any experience of its properties, and beyond that experience how vain is argument! cannot create, it can only perceive." And he concludes "It is infinitely improbable that the cause of mind, that is, of existence, is similar to mind." Be it observed, however, that Shelley does not dogmatise. He simply cannot conceive that mind is the *basis* of all things. The cause of life is still obscure. "All recorded generations of mankind," Shelley says, "have wearily busied themselves in inventing answers to this question ; and the result has been—Religion."

Shelley's essay "On a Future State" follows the same line of reasoning as his essay "On Life." He considers it highly probable that *thought* is "no more than the relation between certain parts of that infinitely varied mass, of which the rest of the universe is composed, and which ceases to exist as soon as those parts change their positions with regard to each other." His conclusion is that "the desire to be for ever as we are, the reluctance to a violent and unexperienced change," which is common to man and other living beings, is the "secret persuasion which has given birth to the opinions of a future state."

If we turn to Shelley's published letters we shall find abundant expressions of hostility to and contempt for religion. Those letters may deserve the praise of Matthew Arnold or the censure of Mr. Swinburne ; but, in either case, they may be taken as honest documents, written to all sorts of private friends, and never intended for publication. Byron's letters were passed about freely, and largely written for effect; Shelley's were written under ordinary conditions, and he unbosomed himself with freedom and sincerity.

From one of his early letters we find that he contemplated a translation of the *System of Nature*, which is frequently quoted in the notes to *Queen Mab*. He couples Jehovah and Mammon together as fit for the worship of "those who delight in wickedness and slavery." In a letter to Henry Reveley he pictures God as delighted with his creation of the earth, and seeing it spin round the sun; and imagines him taking out "patents to supply all the suns in space with the same manufacture." When the poet was informed by Ollier that a certain gentleman (it was Archdeacon Hare) hoped he would humble his soul and "receive the spirit into him," Shelley replied: "if you know him personally, pray ask him from me what he means by receiving the *spirit into me;* and (if really it is any good) how one is to get at it." He goes on to say: "I was immeasurably amused by the quotation from Schlegel about the way in which the popular faith is destroyed—first the Devil, then the Holy Ghost, then God the Father. I had written a Lucianic essay to prove the same thing." In the very year of his death, writing to John Gisborne, he girds at the popular faith in God, and with reference to one of its most abhorrent doctrines he exclaims —"As if, after sixty years' suffering here, we were to be roasted alive for sixty million more in hell, or charitably annihilated by a *coup de grâce* of the bungler who brought us into existence at first."—A dozen other quotations from Shelley's letters might be given, all to pretty much the same effect, but the foregoing must suffice.

A thorough analysis of Shelley's poetry, showing the essential Atheism which runs through it from beginning to end, would require more space than we have at our command. We shall therefore simply point out, by means of instances, how indignantly or contemptuously he always refers to religion as the great despot and impostor of mankind.

The *Revolt of Islam* stigmatises "Faith" as "an obscene worm." The sonnet on the Fall of Bonaparte concludes with a reference to "Bloody Faith, the foulest birth of time." Shelley frequently conceives Faith as serpentine and disgusting. In *Rosalind and Helen* he writes—

> Grey Power was seated
> Safely on her ancestral throne;
> And Faith, the Python, undefeated,
> Even to its blood-stained steps dragged on
> Her foul and wounded train.

In the great and splendid *Ode to Liberty* the image undergoes a Miltonic sublimation.

> Like one fierce cloud over a waste of waves
> Hung tyranny; beneath, sat deified
> The sister-pest, congregator of slaves.

Invariably does the poet class religion and oppression together — "Religion veils her eyes: Oppression shrinks aghast."—" Destruction's sceptred slaves, and Folly's mitred brood."—"And laughter fills the Fane, and curses shake the Throne."

Mr. Herbert Spencer writes with learning and eloquence about the Power of the Universe and the Unknowable. Shelley pricked this bubble of speculation in the following passage:

> What is that Power? Some moonstruck sophist stood
> Watching the shade from his own soul upthrown
> Fill Heaven and darken Earth, and in such mood
> The Form he saw and worshipped was his own,
> His likeness in the world's vast mirror shown.

In one verse of the *Ode to Liberty* the poet exclaims:

> O that the free would stamp the impious name
> Of . . . into the dust or write it there.

What is the omitted word? Mr. Swinburne says the only possible word is—God. We agree with him. Anything else would be a ridiculous anti-climax, and quite inconsistent with the powerful description of—

> this foul gordian word,
> Which, weak itself as stubble, can bind
> Into a mass, irrefragably firm,
> The axes and the rods that awe mankind.

"Pope" and "Christ" are alike impossible. With

respect to "mankind" they are but local designations. The word must be universal. It is *God*.

The glorious speech of the Spirit of the Hour, which terminates the third Act of *Prometheus Unbound*—that superb drama of emancipate Humanity—lumps together "Thrones, altars, judgment seats, and prisons," as parts of one gigantic system of spiritual and temporal misrule. Man, when redeemed from falsehood and evil, rejects his books " of reasoned wrong, glozed on by ignorance"; and the veil is torn aside from all " believed and hoped." And what is the result? Let the Spirit of the Hour answer.

> The loathsome mask has fallen, the man remains
> Sceptreless, free, uncircumscribed, but man
> Equal, unclassed, tribeless, and nationless,
> Exempt from awe, worship, degree, the king
> Over himself; just, gentle, wise; but man
> Passionless? no, yet free from guilt or pain,
> Which were, for his will made or suffered them;
> Nor yet exempt, though ruling them like slaves,
> From chance, and death, and mutability,
> The clogs of that which else might oversoar
> The loftiest star of unascended heaven,
> Pinnacled dim in the intense inane.

What a triumphant flight! The poet springs from earth and is speedily away beyond sight—almost beyond conception—like an elemental thing. But his starting-point is definite enough. Man is exempt from awe and worship; from spiritual as well as political and social slavery; king over himself, ruling the anarchy of his own passions. And the same idea is sung by Demogorgon at the close of the fifth Act. The " Earth-born's spell yawns for heaven's despotism," and " Conquest is dragged captive through the deep."

> Love, from its awful throne of patient power
> In the wise heart, from the last giddy hour
>   Of dread endurance, from the slippery steep,
> And narrow verge of crag-like agony, springs
> And folds over the world its healing wings.

> Gentleness, Virtue, Wisdom, and endurance,
> These are the seals of that most firm assurance
>   Which bars the pit over Destruction's strength;
> And if, with infirm hand, Eternity,
> Mother of many acts and hours, should free
>   The serpent that would clasp her with his length,
> These are the spells by which to re-assume
> An empire o'er the disentangled doom.
> To suffer woes which Hope thinks infinite;
> To forgive wrongs darker than death or night;
>   To defy Power, which seems omnipotent;
> To love, and bear; to hope till Hope creates
> From its own wreck the thing it contemplates;
>   Neither to change, nor falter, nor repent;
> This, like thy glory, Titan! is to be
> Good, great and joyous, beautiful and free;
> This is alone Life, Joy, Empire, and Victory!

This is the Atheism of Shelley. Man is to conquer, by love and hope and thought and endurance, his birthright of happiness and dignity. Humanity is to take the place of God.

It has been argued that if Shelley had lived he would have repented the "indiscretions of his youth," and gravitated towards a more "respectable" philosophy. Well, it is easy to prophesy; and just as easy, and no less effectual, to meet the prophet with a flat contradiction. "Might have been" is no better than "might not have been." Was it not declared that Charles Bradlaugh would have become a Christian if he had lived long enough? Was not the same asserted of John Stuart Mill? One was nearly sixty, the other nearly seventy; and we have to wonder what is the real age of intellectual maturity. Only a few weeks before his death, Shelley wrote of Christianity that "no man of sense could think it true." That was his deliberate and final judgment. Had he lived long enough to lose his sense; had he fallen a victim to some nervous malady, or softening of the brain; had he lingered on to a more than ripe (a rotten) old age, in which senility may unsay the virile words of manhood; it is conceivable that Shelley might have become a devotee of the faith he had despised. But none of these things did happen. What Shelley *was* is the only object of sane discussion. And what he was we know—an Atheist, a lover of Humanity.

LONG FACES.

EVERY one who has turned over old volumes of sermons, adorned with the authors' portraits, must have been struck with the length of their faces. They seem to say—parodying the famous line of Dante—"Abandon jokes all ye who enter here." Those men preached a solemnly absurd creed, and they looked absurdly solemn. Their faces seemed as devoid of merriment as the faces of jackasses, and the heads above them were often as stupid. Justice forbid that I should run down a Hooker, a Barrow, a Taylor, or a South. They were men of *genius*, and all genius is of the blood royal. I read their writings with pleasure and profit, which is more than nine-tenths of the clergy can say with any approach to honesty. But a single swallow does not make a summer, and a few men of genius do not elevate a profession. I am perfectly convinced that the great bulk of the preaching fraternity have cultivated a solemn aspect—not perhaps deliberately, but at least instinctively—in order to impose on the ignorant and credulous multitude. The very tone of voice in which they pray, give out hymns, and preach, is *artificial;* in keeping with their artificial ideas and artificial sentiments; which, if they were expressed in natural tones, would excite universal contempt and derision.

Now this solemnity is the best trick in the priest's game. Gravity is always mistaken by the multitude for wisdom. A round-faced merry fellow shall make a bright, sensible speech, and he will be voted frivolous; but a long-faced, saturnine fellow shall utter a string of dull platitudes, and he will be voted a Solon. This is well known to the clergy, who have developed a perfect art of dullness. They talk an infinite deal of nothing, use a multitude of solemn words to hide an absurdity or no meaning at all, and utter the inherited shibboleths of their craft like the august oracles of a recent revelation.

Concede them the advantage of solemnity, or reverence, or whatever else it is called, and you give them the victory at the beginning of the battle. If you pull a long face over their nonsense, the spectators, after all your arguments, will say, "There *must* be something in it, though, for see how *serious* he is." Whereas a light jest and a merry smile will show you are heart-free, and beyond the range of clerical artillery.

I do not pretend, however, that the efforts of Freethought critics should have no background of seriousness. Wit without reason, says Heine, is but a sneeze of the intelligence. But has not wit ever been the keenest weapon of the great emancipators of the human mind? Not the mere plaything of an idle mind in an idle hour, but the coruscating blade to pierce the weak places of folly and imposture. Aristophanes, Lucian, Rabelais, Erasmus, and Voltaire—to take a few great instances—were all serious in aim and intention. They valued truth, goodness, and beauty, as much as the dreariest preachers. But they felt, because of their temperament, that while the dry light of the intellect is suited to the study of science, it is inadequate in the realm of political, social, and religious debate, where everything is steeped in feeling, and hopes and fears strive together, and imagination kindles the very senses into keener play.

After all, perhaps, this word *temperament* is a solution in itself. When Bishop South was taken to task by a brother bishop for his witticisms, he replied, " Do you mean to say that if God had given you any wit you would not have used it ?" Thus is wisdom justified of her children.

My friendly though severe critic, Dr. Coit, who recently discoursed at South-place Institute (or is it Chapel ?) on the National Secular Society in general and myself in particular, could hardly deny that Voltaire was a master of wit, sarcasm, irony, and ridicule. Well, now, let us see what some serious writers have said of this nimble spirit. Robert Browning, in *The Two Poets of Croisic*, thus salutes him :

> Ay, sharpest shrewdest steel that ever stabbed
> To death Imposture through the armor-joints !

Carlyle says " He gave the death-stab to modern superstition," and " it was a most weighty service." Buckle says he " used ridicule, not as the test of truth, but as the scourge of folly," and thus " produced more effect than the gravest arguments could have done." " Nor can any one since the days of Luther be named," says Brougham, " to whom the spirit of free inquiry, nay, the emancipation of the human mind from spiritual tyranny, owes a more lasting debt of gratitude."

There is a story of the manuscript of Harrington's *Oceana* being filched and given to Cromwell, and the sagacious " usurper " returned it saying, " My government is not to be overturned with paper pellets." But the ironical pamphlet, *Killing no Murder*, produced a different effect. Nor did the royal and imperial despots, and their priestly abettors, in the eighteenth century, dread the solemn lovers of freedom. But the winged pen of Voltaire was a different matter. " Bigots and tyrants," says Macaulay, " who had never been moved by the wailing and cursing of millions, turned pale at his name."

If Dr. Coit imagines that Voltaire has lost his

influence in France, I venture to say he is mistaken. The hand of Voltaire is on Renan, and on dozens of living soldiers in the French army of progress. And what man of letters in England—a country abounding in "the oxen of the gods," strong, slow, and stupid—is free from his influence? Carlyle's early essay on Voltaire is a mixture of hatred and admiration. But read the Life of Frederick, and see how the French snake fascinates the Scotch Puritan, until at last he flings every reservation aside, and hails with glowing panegyric the Savior of Calas.

Let me refer Dr. Coit to the delightful preface of a delightful book—Leland's introduction to his fine translation of Heine's *Reisebilder*. "Woe to those who are standing near," says Leland, "when a humorist of this stamp is turned loose upon the world. He knows nothing of your old laws,—like an Azrael-Napoleon he advances conscienceless, feeling nothing but an overpowering impulse, as of some higher power which bids him strike and spare not." But, after all, the main cause of progress is *agitation*, and though the agitation may be "eminently disagreeable to many, even friends, who are brought within its immediate action, it will be eminently beneficial in the end."

Yes, the hard-bound human mind, like the hard-bound soil, has to be ploughed up. Let it shriek as it will, the work must be done, or the light and air will never penetrate, and an ocean of seeds will lie barren on the surface.

Dr. Coit need not fear that ridicule will excite apprehensions about the multiplication table. Ridicule has a fine scent for its proper prey. It must detect the *ridiculous* before it couches and springs. Truth, honor, consistency, disinterestedness, are invulnerable. What ridicule can kill deserves to die.

Mr. George Meredith writes of "that first-born of common-sense, the vigilant Comic, which is the genius of thoughtful laughter." Folly is the natural prey of this hunter, and Folly is found in the churches as well as in the streets. Some men, however, are non-laughers by birthright, and as men are apt to make a virtue of their deficiencies, it is not surprising if, as Mr. Meredith observes, the "laughter-hater soon learns to dignify this dislike as an objection in morality."

Persons who have read the *Freethinker* from the first do not need to be assured of the earnest spirit of its conductors. They fight no less sternly for the iridescent jewels in their swords. But Dr. Coit appears to object to fighting altogether. He seems to bid us rest content with what we have won. That is, he bids us leave superstition, with all its brood of lies and wrongs, in possession of the schools, the universities, the churches, the hospitals, the workhouses, and every other institution. He bids us leave it with its large grasp on the private and public life of the community, and go on with our constructive work in face of all this overwhelming frustration. No doubt he means well, but we are not foolish enough to take his advice. We tell Dr. Coit that he does not understand the obstructive power of theology, and that he is thus unable to appreciate the work of the National Secular Society.

But let us return to the point of ridicule, and the point of "blasphemy." Dr. Coit found two "lessons for the day" in my *Philosophy of Secularism*, and he spoke of my *Shadow of the Sword* as "a noble plea for peace." But he complained of my exposing the absurdities and immoralities of the Bible—a book which is thrust into the hands of little children in our public schools. He also complained of my dragging to light the Crimes of Christianity. But his anger was most excited by one of my "Bible Romances"—*A Virgin Mother*. Some fastidious persons even object to the title, thus showing their abysmal ignorance of Christian literature. The phrase is common in Catholic books of devotion, like the Mother of God. It occurs in Milton's Ode on the Nativity and in *Paradise Lost*. I have marked it a dozen times in Professor Palgrave's collection of Sacred Songs. But Dr. Coit objects to my comparison of the Holy Ghost's "overshadowing" of the Virgin Mary with the divine impregnations of earthly women by the gods of the Greek pantheon. He regards the one as a "mystery" and the others as vulgar amours. But this depends on your point of view. Lord Bacon found a mine of hidden wisdom in some of these "amours," and Mr. Morris makes beautiful poetry of the loves of Zeus and Danae, which is more than any one has ever succeeded in doing with the relations between the Holy Ghost and Mary. I admit, however, that taste is not disputable; and I refer Dr. Coit to the passage of my *Virgin Mother* in which I cite Justin Martyr as appealing to the Pagans not to mock at the Incarnation, on the express ground that they also taught the same doctrine in their stories of the demi-gods who were born of women after the embraces of deities. Surely, then, it is idle to complain of *my* disrespect of this Christian dogma. Nor is it just to say that my criticism of it cannot be read to a mixed audience. That is the fault of the *doctrine*. So far as my *words* go, there is not a syllable to shock any but a prurient modesty.

With respect to Dr. Coit's plea for bringing the kindness of social intercourse into the war of ideas, I have this to say—It is impossible. Timid persons have always sighed for this policy, but when the fight began they have found themselves "between the fell incensèd points of mighty opposites." Religion should be treated as freely as other subjects. That is all I claim, and I will not be satisfied with less. I cannot consent to relinquish any weapon that is legitimate in other warfare. Nor for the sake of temporary *feeling* will I be false to the permanent *interests* of my species. I will laugh at folly, scorn hypocrisy, expose falsehood, and bathe my sword in the heart's blood of imposture. But I will not descend to personalities. I do not war with *persons*, but with *principles*.

My object is to destroy the Christian superstition and prepare the way for a more rational and humane condition of society. I shall adapt myself, as well as I can, to the shifting conditions of the struggle. My aim is to *succeed*. My policy, therefore, will never be determined by a personal preference. I shall follow the path that promises victory. But I do not, and will not, dictate to others. Within the scope of our principles there is room for many policies. Let each do his best, according to his light and opportunity. Let Dr. Coit, too, go his way as I go mine. We travel by different routes, but perhaps we shall meet at the goal.

OUR FATHER.

God's in his heaven,
All's right with the world.
—R. BROWNING, *Pippa Passes.*

THE Apostles' Creed, with which the Apostles never had anything to do, begins with the words " I believe in God the Father Almighty." The last word, " Almighty," is an adjective which we owe to the metaphysical genius of Christian theologians; and the first words, " I believe," are the customary shibboleth of the priests of every religion. For the rest, this extract from the Creed is taken from the Lord's Prayer, which itself is a brief selection from common Jewish prayers before the days of Jesus. According to the evangelists—whoever *they* were—Jesus taught his disciples to pray to " Our Father which art in Heaven " for a number of things which no one ever obtained by that process. Nevertheless the petition is offered up, generation after generation, by millions of Christians, whose hands are first folded in the gesture of prayer on their mothers' knees, and whose lips are taught at the same time a form of words that clings to them for life.

Our Father! The words are pretty and touching. When the child hears them he thinks of some one like his own father, but immensely bigger and more powerful; and as the child is taught that all the necessaries and comforts of life he enjoys, at the expense of his parents' labor and loving care, are really gifts from the Father behind the scenes, it is no wonder that this mysterious being becomes the object of gratitude and affection.

Which art in Heaven! Up there in the region of dreams, beyond the sailing clouds, far away through the deep blue, where imagination builds its fairy palace of delight, and God sits on his golden throne, and swift, bright angels speed forth to execute his commands. Tell a child anything you please about that land of fancy and you will be believed, especially if the tale comes from beloved lips, or from lips that bear the glamor of authority. And what the child is to the adult, early or savage man is to the civilisee. To the African negroes the highest god is the Sky; the great deity *Dyu* of our Aryan ancestors was the Sky; the Greek *Zeus* and the Latin *Jupiter* were both the Heaven-Father; and we still say " Heaven forgive me!" or " Fear the vengeance of Heaven!"

This Heaven, however, is no longer credible to any one with a tincture of science. Hard as the truth to a child or a savage, the sky is not a reality, but an optical illusion. For forty or forty-five miles from the earth's surface there is a belt of atmosphere, growing rarer and rarer as it approaches the infinite ocean of æther. Gone for ever is the old delusion of a solid Heaven overhead, with windows in it, through which God and the angels looked down upon the earth and its inhabitants. And what site is there for Heaven out in the cold blackness of space?

That Heaven is gone, and where is Our Father? Science shows us a world of absolute order, in which what we call the laws of nature—the observed sequence and recurrence of phenomena—are never broken. The world was not fashioned for man's dwelling, nor is it maintained for his benefit. Towards the poles he freezes, towards the equator he burns. The rain nourishes his crops or rots them, without asking his pleasure; the sea bears him or drowns him, with equal unconcern; the lightning slays him or spares him, whether good, bad or indifferent, as he happens to be in or out of the line of its dazzling flight; famine pinches his cheeks if he cannot procure food; the pestilence seizes upon his nerves and blood unless he learns the antidote to its ravages. He stands amidst the play of terrific forces, and only preserves himself by vigilance, patience, courage and industry. If he falls the enemy is upon him, and the doom of the vanquished is death. Nature shows him no mercy. His mistakes are as fatal as his crimes.

"God" has been in his "Heaven" for eternity, but all is *not* right with the world. Man is always endeavoring to improve it, but what assistance comes from above? A Father in Heaven would be a glorious fact. But who can believe it? "Our Father" is utterly careless of his children. The celestial Rousseau sends all his offspring to the Foundling.

The late hard weather has thrown thousands of honest men out of employment, and increased the death-rate alarmingly. Where is the wisdom of this? Where is the goodness? The worst of men would alter it if they could. But God, they say, can do it, and he does not. Yet they still look up and say "Our Father." And the Father looks down with a face as blenchless as the Sphinx's, gazing forthright across the desert sands.

What father would permit in his family the gross

disparities we see in human life? One gorges and another starves; one is bloated and another is death's counterfeit; one is dressed in three-piled velvet and another goes in looped and windowed rags; one is idle and another slaves; one is sated with pleasure and another is numbed with pain; one lolls in a palace and another shivers in a hovel. What human father would not be ashamed to treat his children with such infamous partiality?

Look at the physical and moral filth, and the mental abasement, in our great Christian cities, where new churches are constantly built for the worship of God, where Bibles are circulated by the million, and where hundreds of sleek gentlemen flourish on the spoils of philanthropy. Read Mr. Rudyard Kipling's story of East-end life; read the lucubrations of General Booth; listen to the ever-swelling wail over the poverty, misery, and degradation of hosts of our people; and then say if it is not high time to cease all this cant about Our Father which art in Heaven.

Man has always been his own Savior. His instrument is science, his wisdom is self-help. His redemption begins when he turns his eyes from the delusive Heaven and plucks up his heart from the fear of Hell. Despair vanishes before the steady gaze of instructed courage. Hope springs as a flower in the path of endeavor.

WAIT TILL YOU DIE.

PASCAL remarked that, whether Christianity were true or false, the Christian was on the safe side; and Diderot replied that the priests and apologists of Mohammedanism, or any other creed, could say the very same thing with equal force. The argument, if it be an argument, implies the possibility of error, and what applies to one religion applies to all. The votaries of every creed may be mistaken if there is no absolute certitude; or, if there should be one true religion among the multitude, and but one, only the devotees of that single faith can be on the safe side. But as no one knows *which* is the only true religion, it follows, according to the law of probabilities, that the odds are greatly against any particular religion being the right one. The Christian therefore would have one chance of being right, and nine hundred and ninety-nine chances of being wrong. He has thus one chance in a thousand above the Atheist.

But, on the other hand, if all religions but one are certainly wrong, what is the chance of a single one being certainly right? Does not the Christian's slight percentage of safety fade into something quite inappreciable in the light of this question? And is what is left—if *anything* is left—an adequate price for the abnegation of manhood? Would it tempt an honest man, with a sense of human dignity, to play fast and loose with his intellect, and accept a creed because it appeals to his selfish hopes and fears? Could such a slender chance of profit in the next life compensate for slavery in this life?

If belief is the safe side, the proper course is to believe *everything*. And it is useless to cry that this is impossible. Faith enables men to believe against reason, and one act of credulity is little easier than a thousand. He whose creed is determined by his fears should give free scope to such emotions. If they are his guides let him follow them. Why should he argue when argument may mislead? Why should he stumble at trifles when he has surmounted the first great obstacle to credulity? Let him believe all the religions of the world at once. He can do this as easily as he can believe in the Trinity. And having embraced all, he may rest satisfied that if there be a true religion he undoubtedly possesses it.

We do not suppose, however, that this reasoning will have any effect on Christians, Buddhists, Brahmins, Mohammedans, or Jews. But that very fact shows the hollow character of the argument from which we started. When the Christian talks about the safe side he is only displaying the weakness of his faith, and appealing to timidity when he has no further appeal to reason.

The argument of "the safe side" would have no pertinency, even with the imbecile, if man were immortal. It seeks advantage from the fact that every man must die. It tries to paralyse reason with the clutch of fear.

How frequent is the superstitionist's remark, "Wait till you come to die!" He does not always use these very words, but this is the meaning of all his verbiage. He forgets, or does not know, that philosophy destroys the terror of death. A rational man is aware of the truth expressed by Mill, that death is but one incident in life, and often the least important. He recognises with Bacon that we die daily. He knows that every hour is a step towards death. He does not play, like an ostrich, with the universal law of mortality; nor, on the other hand, does he allow the tomb to cast its chill obscurity over the business and pleasure of life. He lives without hypocrisy, and when the time comes he will die without fear. As Hamlet says, "the readiness is all." Another word also comes from the wisest of men—" Cowards do often taste of death; the valiant die but once."

A belief that will do for life will do for death. The religionists prove this themselves. Whatever a man is confident of is sustaining. The Christian dies a Christian, and the Mohammedan a Mohammedan. The one has dying visions of angels—or may be of devils; the other sees heaven burst open, and the black-eyed houris of paradise beckon him with rosy fingers. What they leaned on in life supports them in death. Its truth or falsity makes no difference at that moment.

Freethinkers are sustained by *convictions*. Intellect and emotion concur in their case. They have no visions of angels or devils, but dear loved faces are better than phantoms, and he who has done a little good in the world, however humbly and obscurely, may dream of the happier and nobler days to come, when true words and good deeds will have brought forth the glorious fruit of happiness for the children of men.

We do not mean to assert that no Freethinker, at any time, ever relapsed on his death-bed. Such cases have apparently occurred during life, and while one particular religion is in the ascendant it is not difficult to understand them. The relapses are always to the creed a man finds about him, or to the creed of his childhood. They simply prove the power of environment and early training, and that a man needs all his strength to stand against big majorities. At best they are cases of mental pathology.

Great historic Freethinkers have always died true to their convictions. They were used to standing alone. For ample proof of this the reader is referred to my *Infidel Death Beds*. And when smaller Freethinkers are numerous enough they avoid the greatest danger of physical weakness. It is easy for Christian relatives or friends to pester a dying Freethinker; it is easy even, in the worst moments of weakness, to put words in his mouth. But if Freethought friends visit him, he feels strengthened and relieved. Allies may well be needed, sometimes, in such a battle with bigotry.

After all, "Wait till you die!" is an argument of folly and cowardice. What can we conjecture of any other life except from our experience of this? On this earth reason is the safe side, honesty is the safe side, humanity is the safe side; and what is the safe side here is likely to be the safe side elsewhere.

DEAD THEOLOGY.

THIS is an age of "series." Every publisher issues one, and the number of them is legion. As far as possible they are written by "eminent hands," as old Jacob Tonson used to call his wretched scribblers in Grub-street garrets. But not every publisher can secure such an eminent hand as a live Archbishop. This has been achieved, however, by Messrs. Sampson, Low, Marston, and Company. Having projected a series of "Preachers of the Age," they were fortunate enough to enlist the Archbishop of Canterbury under their banner. His Grace, as it is etiquette to call him, though his natural name is Edward White Benson, leads off the publishers' attack on the British public with a volume of sermons entitled *Living Theology*. It is well printed on good paper, the binding is appropriate, and the price of three-and-sixpence puts it within the reach of the great middle-class public which cares for such things. We are far from sharing the opinion of a carper who remarked that, as sermons go, this volume is rather dear. Thirteen sermons by an Archbishop! Could any man in his senses expect them for less money? The real wonder is that a man with £15,000 a-year should condescend to publish at all. We ought to feel thankful that he does not charge us a guinea a volume.

Prefixed to the thirteen sermons, at fourpence apiece, including the binding, is an excellent photogravure portrait of the Archbishop. The face is keen and scholarly, and not unpleasant. A noticeable nose, a large fluent mouth, shrewd eyes, and a high well-shaped head, make on the whole an agreeable picture. Something about the features shows the preacher, and something more the ecclesiastic. It is the type, and the best type, of the learned priest. Nobody could look at this portrait and call Edward White Benson a fool. But is any one in danger of doing so? Would not every one admit some ability in the unhereditary recipient of fifteen thousand a year? Parsons are not a brilliant body, but to wriggle, or climb, or rise to the top of the Black Army involves the possession of uncommon faculties.

The Archbishop is seldom eloquent, in the popular sense of the word; but his style has a certain force and color, always within the limits of exquisite breeding. If he consigned you to Gehenna, he would do it with bland graciousness; and if he swore at all, he would swear in Latin. His language in these sermons, as in another volume we noticed a year ago, is pure and nervous, with an etymological reason for every word. Sometimes he is quite felicitous. Now and then he uses metaphor with skill and illumination. The habitual concreteness of his style shows the clearness of his perceptions. Occasionally he is epigrammatic. "Strong enemies," he says in one place, "are better to us than weak friends. They show us our weak points." Finer and higher is another passage in the same sermon—" The yearning of multitudes is not in vain. After yearning comes impulse, volition, movement." It would be difficult, if not impossible, to better this, unless a great poet cast it in the mould of a metaphor.

We confess that, on the whole, we have read the Archbishop's sermons with some pleasure, as well as with much attention. It is to his credit that he defies a superficial reading. We do not expect to find another volume in the series at all comparable with his. Dr. Maclaren, who comes second, is on a lower level, and the next descent to Mr. Price Hughes is a fall into a slough of incapable and reckless sentimentalism.

Living Theology is the title of the Archbishop's volume, but this is a misnomer, for the title belongs only to the first sermon. It misled us in this general application, as it will probably mislead others. We took it to be a setting forth of so much theology as the Archbishop thought *living*, in contradistinction to what he allowed to be *dead*. But we find a very miscellaneous lot of sermons, sometimes rather on Church work than on Church teaching. The title, therefore, is what Walt Whitman would call "a suck and a sell." Yet it is hardly worth while to labor the complaint, for titles are often better than the pages that follow them. Sometimes, indeed, a writer puts all his head into the title, and the rest of the book displays his imbecility. But this cannot be said of the Archbishop.

Another difficulty is this. The Archbishop's sermons are hard for a Freethinker to criticise. He seldom expounds and rarely argues. He addresses an audience who take the fundamentals of Christianity for granted. Yet he lays himself open here and there, and where he does so we propose to meet him.

In the first sermon Dr. Benson is surely going beyond his actual belief in referring to "the earliest race of man, with whom the whole race so nearly passed away." He can scarcely take the early chapters of Genesis literally at this time of day. In the very next sermon he speaks cheerfully of the age of Evolution. That sermom was preached at St. Mary's, Southampton, to the British Association in 1882. It is on "The Spirit of Inquiry." "The Spirit of Inquiry," he says, " is God's spirit working in capable men, to enlarge the measure and the fulness of man's capacity." But if *capable* men are necessary, to say nothing of favorable conditions, the working of God's spirit seems lost in the natural explanation. Still, it is pleasant to find the Archbishop welcoming the Spirit of Inquiry, under any interpretation of its essence; and it may be hoped that he will vote accordingly when the Liberty of Bequest Bill reaches the Upper Chamber. It is also pleasant to read his admission that the Spirit of Inquiry (we keep his capitals) " has made short work not only of the baser religions, but of the baser forms of ours"—to wit, the Christian. Some of those "baser forms" are indicated in the following passage :

"I know not whether any stern or any sensuous religion of heathendom has held up before men's astonished eyes features more appalling or more repulsive than those of the vindictive father, or of the arbitrary distributor of two eternities, or again of the easy compromiser of offences in return for houses and lands. Dreadful shadows under which thousands have been reared."

Dreadful shadows indeed! And not thousands, but countless millions, have been reared under them. Those dreadful shadows were for centuries the universal objects of Christian worship. They still hover over Spurgeon's tabernacle and a host of other houses of God. But they are hateful to Dr. Benson. To him the God of orthodoxy, the God of the Thirty-nine Articles, is dead. He dismisses Predestination, a vindictive God, and Everlasting Torment. He speaks of the very "prison" where Christ is said to have preached after his death, as a place "where spirits surely unlearn many a bias, many a self-wrought blindness, many a heedless error." Hell is therefore a place of purgation, which is certainly an infinite improvement on the orthodox idea of eternal and irremediable woe, however it fall below the conception that the Creator has no right to punish his own failures.

Let the reader note who makes these admissions of the intellectual and moral death of the "baser forms" of Christianity. It is not an irresponsible *franc-tireur* of the Black Army, nor an expelled soldier like Mr. Voysey, nor a resigned soldier like Dr. Momerie. It is the Archbishop of Canterbury, the highest dignitary of the Church of England.

His Grace does not reflect—he cannot afford to reflect—that as the dead theology of to-day was the living theology of the past, so the living theology of to-day may be the dead theology of to-morrow.

The Archbishop still dogmatises, even in this sermon on the Spirit of Inquiry. In opposition to the man of science who knows of no limits to nature, he declares that "There is a *sum* of created things, and therefore a real end (however far off) to what can be known of them." In a certain sense, truly, there *is* an end to what can be known of nature, for human knowledge must ever be relative and not absolute. But the Archbishop's limit is not qualitative in man; it is quantitative in the universe. Herein he goes beyond the bounds of knowledge, and indulges in the very dogmatism for which he reprehends the materialist.

It is dogmatism also to assert that "the soul has every reason to believe itself absolutely eternal." Absolutely is a word of vast significance. How can it apply to "the soul"? Were "the soul" to subsist eternally in the future, it could not be *absolutely* eternal if it once began to be. "Every reason" is also too comprehensive. Dr. Benson may think he has good reasons for "the soul's" immortality, but he must be aware that divines of his own church have held the contrary doctrine.

Before the Spirit of Inquiry, says Dr. Benson, every other religion than Christianity fades away; though he has admitted that some parts of Christianity, the " baser forms," have shared the same fate. Every fresh conquest of the Spirit of Inquiry has " brought out some trait in the character, or some divine conception in the mind of Jesus of Nazareth." This sweeping statement is supported by " three very clearly marked" instances.

The first is that science shows us the unity of life. " The latest discovered laws involve at least this, that the Life of man is one Life." And this is " no more than the scientific verification of what was long ago stated, and by Christians (at least for a while) acted on."

In support of the Christian idea of the Unity of Life the Archbishop cites St. Paul, who once asked in a callous way if God cared for oxen. Had the Archbishop appealed to Jesus he would have found the oracle dumb, or something worse; for the Nazarene distinctly told his apostles to preach only to the Jews, and leave the Samaritans and Gentiles in darkness. St. Paul took a flight beyond this narrow patriotism. It was he, and not the personal disciples of Jesus, who broke down the barriers between Jew and Gentile. It was he who scorned the idea that Jesus, to use his own language, was only sent to the lost sheep of the house of Israel. It was he, and not Peter, or James, or John, who said that God had made all nations of one blood; he who declared "ye are all one in Christ." Yet it is easy to make too much of this; for St. Paul did not include the heathen and unbelievers within the fold of brotherhood; and when he asserted the fatherhood of God, he appealed to the previous utterance of a Greek poet, thus conceding his own want of originality.

One might imagine, too, that the old Jewish story of Creation—which in turn was not original—involved the common descent of the human race; and as this idea was almost, if not quite, universal, being based on the obvious generic resemblance of the various races of mankind, it seems a stretch of fancy to put it forward as "a Christian statement" in some way connected with "Jesus of Nazareth."

The Archbishop's second instance of the concurrence of modern progress with the teaching of Jesus, is, to say the least of it, peculiar. "From the liberty to inquire," he says, "comes the liberty to express the results of inquiry. And this is the preamble of the Charter of Jesus Christ."

We defy Dr. Benson to find a single plain passage about freedom of thought in the teachings of Jesus. The Nazarene was fond of saying, "He that hath ears to hear let him hear." But it was reserved for Ingersoll to say, "He that hath a brain to think let him think."

The Archbishop goes on to claim Darwin as "our aged Master"—Darwin, who rejected Christianity for forty years of his life! He quotes from Beale the sentence, "Intellectual work of every kind must be free." "And the New Testament," he adds, "is still the one volume of books on religion which accepts this whole statement."

This is a bold—some would say a brazen—assertion. If the New Testament teaches anything clearly, it teaches that belief is necessary to salvation. That doctrine stifles free speech and extinguishes inquiry. Why investigate if you may be damned for your conclusions? And why allow investigation if another man's errors may involve your perdition? These questions have been answered logically enough by the Christian Church, and the "Charter of Jesus Christ" has been the worst of spiritual oppressions. No religion has been so intolerant as the Christian. Mohammedanism has been far less bigoted. Buddhism has the proud distinction of never having persecuted one human being in twenty-four centuries.

The Archbishop's third instance is fantastic to the

point of grotesqueness. Both Christianity and the
Spirit of Inquiry, he says, are at one in "the demand
for fruit." Does he mean to imply that other religions
set their faces against "fruit"? Buddhism is quite
imperative about moral duties. Mohammedanism gets
itself obeyed in matters of conduct, while Christianity
is quite ineffectual. Drink, gambling, and prostitution
abound in Christian countries; in the Mohammedan
world they have been sternly repressed. This is
admitted by Dr. Benson in his volume on *Christ and
His Times*; admitted, and even emphasised; so that he
may, as it were, be confuted out of his own mouth.

If we take a leap to the penultimate sermon in the
present volume, we find Archbishop Benson indulging
in the same kind of loose statement and inconse-
quential reasoning. Its title is "Christ's Crucifixion,
an All in All." The preacher scorns the Greek notion
of the Crucifixion as "the shocking martyrdom of a
grand young moralist." Such a notion, he says, is
"quite inconsistent with the facts." Either we know
not what Christ taught, or else he was more than man.
And the Archbishop sets about proving this by means
of a series of leaps over logical chasms.

After dilating on the innocence of Christ, who was
certainly guilty according to the Mosaic law, and
deserving of death according to the express command
of Jehovah, the Archbishop writes as follows:

"Then we look back through our eighteen centuries, and
we see that before the age of three-and-thirty he had fashioned
sayings, had compacted thoughts, had expressed principles
about duty, about the relative worth of things, about life,
about love, about intercourse with God, about the formation of
character, the relation of classes, the spirit of law, the essence
of government, the unity of man, which had not existed, or
which were not formulated when he opened his lips, but which
have been and are the basis of society from the time they were
known till now."

This is a tissue of false assumptions. The sayings,
thoughts, and principles of Jesus *did* exist before, and
they *were* formulated when he opened his lips. Not

one original utterance is ascribed to him in the whole of the Gospels. It is idle to bandy generalisations; let the Archbishop select specimens of Christ's teaching, and we will find parallels to them, sometimes better and more wisely expressed, in the utterances of his predecessors. Nor is it true that Christ's teachings have been, or are, the basis of society. Society exists in defiance of them. It is never based, and it never will be based, on any abstract teaching. Its basis is *self-interest*, ever increasing in complexity, and ever more and more illuminated by the growth of knowledge.

Take the case of oaths. Jesus said plainly, " Swear not at all." But when earthly potentates wanted their subjects to swear fidelity, the Christian priests discovered that Jesus meant, " Swear only on special occasions." And it was reserved for an Atheist, in the nineteenth century, to pass an Act allowing Christians to obey Jesus Christ.

Take the injunction, " Lay not up for yourselves treasures on earth." Society could never exist upon such a basis, so the clergy find that Jesus, like Polonius, spoke tropically. Every Christian is busy laying up treasures on earth, and Archbishop Benson is well to the front in the competition.

Having made ridiculous claims for Jesus Christ, the Archbishop proceeds in this wise: " Next ask yourself whether a stainless, loving, sincere, penetrating person like that makes or enlarges on unfounded declarations as to matters of fact. Is it consistent with such a character?" Now Jesus speaks of " the immense importance of his own person," he speaks of " My flesh, My blood " as of vital power, he says " I and my Father are one." Could he have been deceived? Well, why not? Honesty does not guarantee us against error. The best of men have been mistaken, And sincere natures are most liable to be deceived by taking subjective impressions for external realities.

There is another explanation which the Archbishop

is too shrewd to pass over in silence. Perhaps others said those things for Jesus, perhaps they "attributed to him sayings which he did not utter." But this, the Archbishop says, only multiplies the difficulty and the astonishment; for, to put it briefly, his biographers in that case were as good at predicting and inventing as himself. And why not? Do we not know that the story of the woman taken in adultery, which is finely told, and has all along been thought to contain some of Christ's most characteristic teaching, does not exist in the earlier manuscripts? It was invented by an unknown writer. And if one unknown writer could (and did) invent this story, other unknown writers may have invented every part of the Gospel narratives.

The attempt to make Jesus sponsor for himself is the last refuge of hard-driven Christians. The frame of mind it evinces is seen in Dr. Benson's interpretation of the exclamation "I thirst," ascribed to Jesus on the cross. Crucifixion produced an intolerable thirst, and the exclamation is very natural; but Dr. Benson says that Jesus meant "I thirst for souls," and and adds that "no man can doubt" it. Such are the shifts to which Christians are reduced when they cling to faith in defiance of reason.

Dr. Benson's "living theology" is dead theology. It is sentimentalism and make-believe. Perfectly scriptural doctrines are cast aside while others are arbitrarily retained. Vague talk about "Christ and him crucified" takes the place of time-honored dogmas, logically deduced from the "Word of God," and stamped with the deliberate approval of councils and synods. Christianity, in short, is becoming a matter of personal taste and preference. The time is approaching when every Christian will have a Christianity of his own.

This is the moral of the Archbishop's volume. Had space permitted we should have liked to notice other features of his sermons. In one place he says that "the so-called Secularist is the man who deprives things secular of all power and meaning and beauty." We think that he deprives Christianity of all meaning, and that being gone its "power" and "beauty" are idle themes of wasted eloquence.

MR. GLADSTONE ON DEVILS.

When the Grand Old Man crossed swords with Professor Huxley on the miracle of Gadara, he spent all his time in discussing whether the pigs belonged to Jews or Gentiles. The more serious point, whether a legion of devils were actually cast out of one or two men and sent into a herd of swine, he sedulously avoided. Professor Huxley, however, is too wide-awake to be drawn off the scent; and while he disputed the points of geography and ethnology, he insisted upon the fact that their only importance was their relation to a miraculous story, which marked the parting of the ways between Science and Christianity.

The demonic theory of disease, including insanity, is universal among savages. For proof and illustration the reader has only to consult Dr. Tylor's splendid work on *Primitive Culture*. There are special demons for every malady, and the way to cure the disease is to cast out the evil spirit. Of course insanity is a striking disorder, and in default of the pathological explanation the savage regards the wild, wandering words and inexplicable actions of the sufferer as the words and actions of a demon, who has taken possession of the man's body, and driven his soul abroad or put it in abeyance. This theory of madness survived through all the centuries of Christian history until the advent of modern science. Mad people were chained up, exhibited as objects of derision, and often beaten unmercifully. It was the *devil* in them, as in the poor witches, that was treated in this fashion. And it was a recognised part of a clergyman's business to cast out devils. The Church of England canon is still unrepealed which provides that the clergy, before engaging in this useful if not agreeable occupation, must obtain the written authority of their bishops.

Laugh or smile as we will at this superstition, it is an integral part of the New Testament. The demonic theory of disease is confessed in the story of Jesus rebuking the fever of Peter's mother-in-law, so that it left her instantaneously, flying out of the door or window, or up the chimney. Jesus repeatedly cast out devils. He expelled seven, in succession or at one fell swoop, from Mary Magdalene. He turned a legion—that is, several thousands—out of the possessed Gadarenes; there being at least one apiece for the bedevilled swine who were driven to destruction. Paul likewise cast out devils. Indeed, if demonic possession in the New Testament is explained away, there is no reason why every other miraculous element should not be dealt with in the same manner.

Mr. Gladstone perceives this, although he does not commit himself in his *Impregnable Rock of Holy Scripture*. "I am afraid," he says, in a letter to the Rev. J. W. Belcher, " that the objections to demoniacal possession involve in germ the rejection of all belief in the supernatural." This is wonderfully clear and straightforward for the Grand Old Man. Give up the belief that mad people may be tenanted by devils, and and you should immediately join the National Society Society. You have taken the first decisive step on the broad road of "infidelity," and nothing but a want of logic or courage prevents you from hastening to the inevitable conclusion.

Archbishop Trench, in his *Notes on the Miracles of*

Our Lord, rejects the theory that the "demoniacs" were simply insane. No doubt, he says, there was "a substratum of disease, which in many cases helped to lay open the sufferer to the deeper evil." But "our Lord Himself uses language which is not reconcileable" with the naturalist theory. "It may well be a question moreover," says Trench, "if an Apostle, or one with apostolic discernment of spirits, were to enter now into one of our madhouses, how many of the sufferers there he might not recognise as thus having more immediately fallen under the tyranny of the powers of darkness."

Dean Milman, the discreet, plausible, and polished historian of the Christian superstition, did not shrink from regarding the New Testament demoniacs as merely insane; and "nothing was more probable," he remarked, "than that lunacy should take the turn and speak the language of the prevailing superstition of the times." Precisely so. But why did Jesus imitate the lunatics? He addresses the evil spirit and not the madman. "Hold thy peace," he says, "and come out of him." No doubt the demoniacs were simply insane; but in that case Jesus himself was mistaken, or the evangelists put into his mouth words that he never used. The first alternative destroys the divinity of Jesus; the second destroys the authority of the evangelists.

Mr. Gladstone's position is the only honest and logical one for a professed Christian. Demonic possession cannot be cut out of the New Testament without leaving a gap through which all the "infidelity" in the world might pass freely. Devils are not confined to hell. They are commercial travellers in brimstone and mischief. They go home occasionally; the rest of the time they are abroad on business. When they see a promising madman they get inside him, and find warmer quarters than the universal air. Very likely they have started Theosophy, in order to provide themselves with fresh residences.

Little devils of course involve the big Devil—Apollyon, Beelzebub, Abaddon, Satan, Lucifer, Old Nick. He commands the infernal armies, and is one of the deities in Mr. Gladstone's pantheon. He is even embedded in the revised version of the Lord's Prayer—like a fly in amber. "Deliver us from evil" now reads "Deliver us from the Evil One." Thus the Devil triumphs, and the first of living English statesmen is reduced by Christian superstition to the level of modern savages and ancient barbarians. Mr. Gladstone is perhaps the highest type of the Christian statesman. But how small and effeminate he appears, after all, in comparison with a great Pagan statesman like Julius Cæsar, whose brain was free from all superstition! Were the "mighty Julius" to re-appear on earth, and see a great statesman believing the story of devils being turned out of men into pigs, he would wonder what blight had fallen upon the human intellect in two thousand years.

HUXLEY'S MISTAKE.

No one will suspect us of any prejudice against Professor Huxley. We have often praised his vigorous writings, and his admirable service to Freethought. We recognise him as a powerful fighter in the great battle between Reason and Faith. He is a born controversialist, he revels in the vivisection of a theological opponent, and it is easy to understand how the more placid Darwin could cry to him admiringly, "What a man you are!"

But for some reason or other it seems the fate of Professor Huxley, as it is the fate of Herbert Spencer, to be made use of by the enemies of Freethought; and it must be admitted that, to a certain extent, he gratuitously plays into their hands.

Mr. Herbert Spencer has been a perfect god-send to the Christians with his " Unknowable "—the creation of which was the worst day's work he ever accomplished. It is only a big word, printed with a capital letter, to express the objective side of the relativity of human knowledge. It connotes all that we do not know. It is a mere confession of ignorance; it is hollowness, emptiness, a vacuum, a nothing. And this nothing, which Mr. Spencer adorns with endless quasi-scientific rhetoric, is used as a buttress to prop up tottering Churches.

Professor Huxley has been nearly as serviceable to the Churches with his " Agnosticism," which belongs to the same category of substantially meaningless terms as the " Unknowable." No doubt it serves the turn of a good many feeble sceptics. It sounds less offensive than " Atheism." An Agnostic may safely be invited to dinner, while an Atheist would pocket the spoons. But this pandering to "respectability" is neither in the interest of truth nor in the interest of character. An Atheist is without God; an Agnostic does not know anything about God, so he is without God too. They come to the same thing in the end. An Agnostic is simply an Atheist with a tall hat on. Atheism carries its own name at the Hall of Science; when it occupies a fine house at Eastbourne, and moves in good society, it calls itself Agnosticism. And then the Churches say, " Ah, the true man of science shrinks from Atheism; he is only an Agnostic; he stands reverently in the darkness, waiting for the light."

Nor is this the only way in which Professor Huxley has helped " the enemy." He is, for instance, far too fond of pressing the " possibility " of miracles. We have no right, he says, to declare that miracles are impossible; it is asserting more than we know, besides begging the question at issue. Perfectly true. But Professor Huxley should remember that he uses "possibility" in one sense and the theologians in another. He uses it theoretically, and they use it practically. They use it where it has a meaning, and he uses it where it has no meaning at all, except in an *à priori* way, like a pair of brackets with nothing between them. When the Agnostic speaks of the "possibility" of miracles, he only means that we cannot prove a universal negative.

Let us take an instance. Suppose some one asserts that a man can jump over the moon. No one can demonstrate that the feat is impossible. It is *possible*, in the sense that *anything* is possible. But this is theoretical logic. According to practical logic it is impossible, in the sense that no rational man would take a ticket for the performance.

Why then does Professor Huxley press the "possibility" of miracles against his Freethinking friends? He is not advancing a step beyond David Hume. He is merely straining logical formulæ in the interest of the Black Army.

Now let us take another instance. In a recent letter to the *Times*, with respect to the famous letter of the thirty-eight clergymen who have given the Bible a fresh certificate, Professor Huxley is once more careful to point out that science knows nothing of " the primal origin " of the universe. But who ever said that it did? Atheists, at any rate, are not aware that the universe ever *had* an origin. As to the " ultimate cause of the evolutionary process," it seems to us mere metaphysical jargon, as intolerable as anything in the sounding phraseology of the theologians.

But this is not all. Professor Huxley delivers himself of the following utterance : " In fact it requires some depth of philosophical incapacity to suppose that there is any logical antagonism between Theism and the doctrine of Evolution." This is food and drink to a paper like the *Christian World*. But what does it mean? Certainly there is no antagonism between the terms " Theism " and " Evolution." They do not fight each other in the dictionary. But is there not antagonism between Evolution and any kind of Theism yet formulated? The word " God " means anything or nothing. Give your God attributes, and see if they are consistent with Evolution. That is the only way to decide whether there is any " logical antagonism " between Evolution and Theism. The trouble begins when you are " logical " enough to deal in definitions; and the only definition of God that will stand the test of Evolution is " a sort of a something."

We leave Professor Huxley to present that highly edifying Theistic conclusion to his old theological opponents, and, if he likes, to flaunt it in the faces of his Freethinking friends. But is it really worth while for Samson to grind chaff for the Philistines? We put the question to Professor Huxley with all seriousness. Let him teach truth and smite falsehood, without spending so much time in showing that they harmonise when emptied of practical meaning. A sovereign and a feather fall with equal rapidity in a vacuum; and if you take away fact and experience, one proposition is as " possible " as another. But why should a great man waste his energies in propagating such a barren truism?

THE GOSPEL OF FREETHOUGHT.

CHRISTIANS are perpetually crying that we destroy and never build up. Nothing could be more false, for all negation has a positive side, and we cannot deny error without affirming truth. But even if it were true, it would not lessen the value of our work. You must clear the ground before you can build, and plough before you sow. Splendor gives no strength to an edifice whose foundations are treacherous, nor can a harvest be reaped from fields unprepared for the seed.

Freethought is, in this respect, like a skilful physician, whose function it is to expel disease and leave the patient sound and well. No sick man claims that the doctor shall supply him with something in place of his malady. It is enough that the enemy of his health is driven out. He is then in a position to act for himself. He has legs to walk with, a brain to devise, and hands to execute his will. What more does he need? What more can he ask without declaring himself a weakling or a fool? So it is with superstition, the deadliest disease of the mind. Freethought casts it out, with its blindness and its terrors, and leaves the mind clear and free. All nature is then before us to study and enjoy. Truth shines on us with celestial light, Goodness smiles on our best endeavors, and Beauty thrills our senses and kindles our imagination with the subtle magic of her charms.

What a boon it is to think freely, to let the intellect dart out in quest of truth at every point of the compass, to feel the delight of the chase and the gladness of capture! What a noble privilege to pour treasures of knowledge into the alembic of the brain, and separate the gold from the dross!

The Freethinker takes nothing on trust, if he can help it; he dissects, analyses, and proves everything. Does this make him a barren sceptic? Not so. What he discards he knows to be worthless, and he also knows the value of what he prizes. If one sweet vision turns out a mirage, how does it lessen our enjoyment at the true oasis, or shake our certitude of water and shade under the palm-trees by the well?

The masses of men do not think freely. They scarcely think at all out of their round of business. They are trained not to think. From the cradle to the grave orthodoxy has them in its clutches. Their religion is settled by priests, and their political and social institutions by custom. They look askance at the man who dares to question what is established, not reflecting that all orthodoxies were once heterodox, that without innovation there could never have been any progress, and that if inquisitive fellows had not gone prying about in forbidden quarters ages ago, the world would still be peopled by savages dressed in nakedness, war-paint, and feathers. The mental stultification which begins in youth reaches ossification as men grow older. Lack of thought ends in incapacity to think.

Real Freethought is impossible without education. The mind cannot operate without means or construct without materials. Theology opposes education: Freethought supports it. The poor as well as the rich should share in its blessings. Education is a social capital which should be supplied to all. It enriches and expands. It not only furnishes the mind, but strengthens its faculties. Knowledge is power. A race of giants could not level the Alps; but ordinary men, equipped with science, bore through their base, and make easy channels for the intercourse of divided nations.

Growth comes with use, and power with exercise. Education makes both possible. It puts the means of salvation at the service of all, and prevents the faculties from moving about *in vacuo*, and finally standing still from sheer hopelessness. The educated man has a whole magazine of appliances at his command, and his intellect is trained in using them, while the uneducated man has nothing but his strength, and his training is limited to its use.

Freethought demands education for all. It claims a mental inheritance for every child born into the world. Superstition demands ignorance, stupidity, and degradation. Wherever the schoolmaster is busy, Freethought prospers; where he is not found, superstition reigns supreme and levels the people in the dust.

Free speech and Freethought go together. If one is hampered the other languishes. What is the use of thinking if I may not express my thought? We claim equal liberty for all. The priest shall say what he believes and so shall the sceptic. No law shall protect the one and disfranchise the other. If any man disapproves what I say, he need not hear me a second time. What more does he require? Let him listen to what he likes, and leave others to do the same. Let us have justice and fair play all round.

Freethought is not only useful but laudable. It involves labor and trouble. Ours is not a gospel for those who love the soft pillow of faith. The Freethinker does not let his ship rot away in harbor; he spreads his canvas and sails the seas of thought. What though tempests beat and billows roar? He is undaunted, and leaves the avoidance of danger to the sluggard and the slave. He will not pay their price for ease and safety. Away he sails with Vigilance at the prow and Wisdom at the helm. He not only traverses the ocean highways, but skirts unmapped coasts and ventures on uncharted seas. He gathers spoils in every zone, and returns with a rich freight that compensates for all hazards. Some day or other, you say, he will be shipwrecked and lost. Perhaps. All things end somehow. But if he goes down he will die like a man and not like a coward, and have for his requiem the psalm of the tempest and the anthem of the waves.

Doubt is the beginning of wisdom. It means caution, independence, honesty and veracity. Faith means negligence, serfdom, insincerity and deception. The man who never doubts never thinks. He is like a straw in the wind or a waif on the sea. He is one of the helpless, docile, unquestioning millions, who keep the world in a state of stagnation, and serve as a fulcrum for the lever of despotism. The stupidity of the people, says Whitman, is always inviting the insolence of power.

Buckle has well said that scepticism is " the necessary antecedent of all progress." Without it we should still be groping in the night of the Dark Ages. The very foundations of modern science and philosophy were laid on ground which was wrested from the Church, and every stone was cemented with the blood of martyrs. As the edifice arose the sharpshooters of faith attacked the builders at every point, and they still continue their old practice, although their missiles can hardly reach the towering heights where their enemies are now at work.

Astronomy was opposed by the Church because it unsettled old notions of the earth being the centre of the universe, and the sun, moon, and stars mere lights stuck in the solid firmament, and worked to and fro like sliding panels. Did not the Bible say that General Joshua commanded the sun to stand still, and how could this have happened unless it moved round the earth? And was not the earth certainly flat, as millions of flats believed it to be? The Catholic Inquisition forced Galileo to recant, and Protestant Luther called Copernicus " an old fool."

Chemistry was opposed as an impious prying into the secrets of God. It was put in the same class with sorcery and witchcraft, and punished in the same way. The early chemists were regarded as agents of the Devil, and their successors are still regarded as " uncanny" in the more ignorant parts of Christendom. Roger Bacon was persecuted by his brother monks; his testing fire was thought to have come from the pit, and the explosion of his gunpowder was the Devil vanishing in smoke and smell. Even at the end of last century, the clergy-led mob of Birmingham who wrecked Priestley's house and destroyed his apparatus, no doubt felt that there was a close connection between chemistry and infidelity.

Physiology and Medicine were opposed on similar grounds. We were all fearfully and wonderfully made, and the less the mystery was looked into the better. Disease was sent by God for his own wise ends, and to resist it was as bad as blasphemy. Every discovery and every reform was decried as impious. Men now living can remember how the champions of faith denounced the use of anæsthetics in painful labor as an interference with God's curse on the daughters of Eve.

Geology was opposed because it discredited Moses, as though that famous old Jew had watched the deposit of every stratum of the earth's crust. It was even said that fossils had been put underground by God to puzzle the wiseacres, and that the Devil had carried shells to the hill-tops for the purpose of deluding men to infidelity and perdition. Geologists were anathematised from the pulpits and railed at by tub-thumpers. They were obliged to feel their way and go slowly. Sir Charles Lyell had to keep back his strongest conclusions for at least a quarter of a century, and could not say all he thought until his head was whitened by old age and he looked into the face of Death.

Biology was opposed tooth and nail as the worst of all infidelity. It exposed Genesis and put Moses out of court. It destroyed all special creation, showed man's kinship with other forms of life, reduced Adam and Eve to myths, and exploded the doctrine of the Fall. Darwin was for years treated as Antichrist, and Huxley as the great beast. All that is being changed, thanks to the sceptical spirit. Darwin's corpse is buried in

Westminster Abbey, but his ideas are undermining all the churches and crumbling them into dust.

The gospel of Freethought brands persecution as the worst crime against humanity. It stifles the spirit of progress and strangles its pioneers. It eliminates the brave, the adventurous and the aspiring, and leaves only the timid, the sluggish and the grovelling. It removes the lofty and spares the low. It levels all the hills of thought and makes an intellectual flatness. It drenches all the paths of freedom with blood and tears, and makes earth the vestibule of hell.

Persecution is the right arm of priestcraft. The black militia of theology are the sworn foes of Freethought. They represent it as the sin against the Holy Ghost, for which there is no forgiveness in this world or the next. When they speak of the Holy Ghost they mean themselves. Freethought is a crime against *them*. It strips off the mystery that invests their craft, and shows them as they really are, a horde of bandits who levy black mail on honest industry, and preach a despot in heaven in order to maintain their own tyranny on earth.

The gospel of Freethought would destroy all priesthoods. Every man should be his own priest. If a professional soul-doctor gives you wrong advice and leads you to ruin, he will not be damned for you. He will see you so first. We must take all responsibility, and we should also take the power. Instead of putting our thinking out, as we put our washing, let us do it at home. No man can do another's thinking for him. What is thought in the originator is only acquiescence in the man who takes it at secondhand.

If we do our own thinking in religion we shall do it in everything else. We reject authority and act for ourselves. Spiritual and temporal power are brought under the same rule. They must justify themselves or go. The Freethinker is thus a politician and a social reformer. What a Christian *may* be he *must* be. Freethinkers are naturally Radicals. They are almost to a man on the side of justice, freedom and progress. The Tories know this, and hence they seek to suppress us by the violence of unjust law. They see that we are a growing danger to every kind of privilege, a menace to all the idle classes who live in luxury on the sweat and labor of others—the devouring drones who live on the working bees.

The gospel of Freethought teaches us to distinguish between the knowable and the unknowable. We cannot fathom the infinite "mystery of the universe" with our finite plummet, nor see aught behind the veil of death. Here is our appointed province:

> This world which is the world
> Of all of us, and where in the end
> We find our happiness or not at all.

Let us make the best of this world and take our chance of any other. If there is a heaven, we dare say it will hold all honest men. If it will not, those who go elsewhere will at least be in good company.

Our salvation is here and now. It is certain and not contingent. We need not die before we realise it. Ours is a gospel, and the only gospel, for this side of the grave. The promises of theology cannot be made good till after death; ours are all redeemable in this life.

We ask men to acknowledge realities and dismiss fictions. When you have sifted all the learned sermons ever preached, you will find very little good grain. Theology deals with dreams and phantasies, and gives no guidance to practical men. The whole truth of life may be summed up in a few words. Happiness is the only good, suffering the only evil, and selfishness the only sin. And the whole duty of man may be expressed in one sentence, slightly altered from Voltaire—Learn what is true in order to do what is right. If a man can tell you anything about these matters, listen to him; if not, turn a deaf ear, and let him preach to the wind.

The only noble things in this world are great hearts and great brains. There is no virtue in a starveling piety which turns all beauty into ugliness and shrivels up every natural affection. Let the heart beat high with courage and enterprise, and throb with warm passion. Let the brain be an active engine of thought, imagination and will. The gospel of sorrow has had its day; the time has come for the gospel of gladness. Let us live out our lives to the full, radiating joy on all in our own circle, and diffusing happiness through the grander circle of humanity, until at last we retire from the banquet of life, as others have done before us, and sink in eternal repose.

ON RIDICULE.

GOLDSMITH said there are two classes of people who dread ridicule—priests and fools. They cry out that it is no argument, but they know it is. It has been found the most potent form of argument. Euclid used it in his immortal Geometry; for what else is the *reductio ad absurdum* which he sometimes employs? Elijah used it against the priests of Baal. The Christian fathers found it effective against the Pagan superstitions, and in turn it was adopted as the best weapon of attack on *them* by Lucian and Celsus. Ridicule has been used by Bruno, Erasmus, Luther, Rabelais, Swift, and Voltaire, by nearly all the great emancipators of the human mind.

All these men used it for a serious purpose. They were not comedians who amused the public for pence.

They wielded ridicule as a keen rapier, more swift and fatal than the heaviest battle-axe. Terrible as was the levin-brand of their denunciation, it was less dreaded than the Greek fire of their sarcasm. I repeat that they were men of serious aims, and indeed how could they have been otherwise? All true and lasting wit is founded on a basis of seriousness; or else, as Heine said, it is nothing but a sneeze of the reason. Hood felt the same thing when he proposed for his epitaph: "Here lies one who made more puns, and spat more blood, than any other man of his time."

Buckle well says, in his fine vindication of Voltaire, that he "used ridicule, not as the test of truth, but as the scourge of folly." And he adds—

"His irony, his wit, his pungent and telling sarcasms, produced more effect than the gravest arguments could have done; and there can be no doubt that he was fully justified in using those great resources with which nature had endowed him, since by their aid he advanced the interests of truth, and relieved men from some of their most inveterate prejudices."

Victor Hugo puts it much better in his grandiose way, when he says of Voltaire that "he was irony incarnate for the salvation of mankind."

Voltaire's opponents, as Buckle points out, had a foolish reverence for antiquity, and they were impervious to reason. To compare great things with small, our opponents are of the same character. Grave argument is lost upon them; it runs off them like water from a duck. When we approach the mysteries of their faith in a spirit of reverence, we yield them half the battle. We must concede them nothing. What they call reverence is only conventional prejudice. It must be stripped away from the subject, and if argument will not remove the veil, ridicule will. Away with the insane notion that absurdity is reverend because it is ancient! If it is thousands of years old, treat it exactly as if it were told the first time to-day. Science recognises nothing in space and time to invalidate the laws of nature. They prevailed in the past as well as in the present, in Jerusalem as well as in London. That is how Science regards everything; and at bottom Science and common-sense are one and the same.

Professor Huxley, in his admirable little book on Hume, after pointing out the improbability of centaurs, says that judged by the canons of science all "miracles" are centaurs. He also considers what would happen if he were told by the greatest anatomist of the age that he had seen a centaur. He admits that the weight of such authority would stagger him, but it would scarcely make him believe. "I could get no further," says Huxley, "than a suspension of judgment."

Now I venture to say that if Johannes Müller had told Huxley any such thing, he would have at once concluded that the great anatomist was joking or suffering from hallucination. As a matter of fact trained investigators do not see these incredible monstrosities, and Huxley's hypothetical case goes far beyond every attested miracle. But I do say that if Johannes Müller, or anyone else, alleged that he had seen a centaur, Huxley would never think of investigating the absurdity.

Yet the allegation of a great anatomist on such a matter is infinitely more plausible than any miraculous story of the Christian religion. The "centaurs" of faith were seen centuries ago by superstitious people; and what is more, the relation of them was never made by the witnesses, but always by other people, who generally lived a few generations at least after the time.

What on earth are we to do with people who believe in "centaurs" on such evidence, who make laws to protect their superstition, and appoint priests at the public cost to teach the "centaur" science? The way to answer this question is to ask another. How should we treat people who believed that centaurs could be seen now? Why, of course, we should laugh at them.

And that is how we should treat people who believe that men-horses ever existed at all.

Does anybody ask that I shall seriously discuss whether an old woman with a divining-rod can detect hidden treasures; whether Mr. Home floated in the air or Mrs. Guppy sailed from house to house; whether cripples are cured at Lourdes or all manner of diseases at Winifred's Well? Must I patiently reason with a man who tells me that he saw water turned into wine, or a few loaves and fishes turned into a feast for multitudes, or dead men rise up from their graves? Surely not. I do what every sensible man does. I recognise no obligation to reason with such hallucinate mortals; I simply treat them with ridicule.

So with the past. Its delusions are no more entitled to respect than those of to-day. Jesus Christ as a miracle-worker is just as absurd as any modern pretender. Whether in the Bible, the Koran, the Arabian Nights, Monte Christo, or Baron Munchausen, a tremendous " walker " is the fit subject of a good laugh. And Freethinkers mean to enjoy their laugh, as some consolation for the wickedness of superstition. The Christian faith is such that it makes us laugh or cry. Are we wrong in preferring to laugh?

There is an old story of a man who was plagued by the Devil. The fiend was always dropping in at inconvenient times, and making the poor fellow's life a hell on earth. He sprinkled holy water on the floor, but by-and-bye the " old 'un " hopped about successfully on the dry spots. He flung things at him, but all in vain. At last he resolved on desperate measures. He plucked up his courage, looked the Devil straight in the face, and laughed at him. That ended the battle. The Devil could not stand laughter. He fled that moment and never returned.

Superstition is the Devil. Treat him to a hearty wholesome laugh. It is the surest exorcism, and you will find laughter medicinal for mind and body too. Ridicule, and again ridicule, and ever ridicule!

WHO ARE THE BLASPHEMERS?

ATHEISTS are often charged with blasphemy, but it is a crime they cannot commit. God is to them merely a word, expressing all sorts of ideas, and not a person. It is, properly speaking, a general term, which includes all that there is in common among the various deities of the world. The idea of the supernatural embodies itself in a thousand ways. Truth is always simple and the same, but error is infinitely diverse. Jupiter, Jehovah, and Mumbo-Jumbo are alike creations of human fancy, the products of ignorance and wonder. Which is *the* God is not yet settled. When the sects have decided this point, the question may take a fresh turn; but until then *god* must be considered as a generic term, like *tree* or *horse* or *man;* with just this difference, however, that while the words tree, horse, and man express the general qualities of visible objects, the word god expresses only the imagined qualities of something that nobody has ever seen.

When the Atheist examines, denounces, or satirises the gods, he is not dealing with persons but with ideas. He is incapable of insulting God, for he does not admit the existence of any such being.

Ideas of god may be good or bad, beautiful or ugly; and according as he finds them the Atheist treats them. If we lived in Turkey, we should deal with the god of the Koran; but as we live in England, we deal with the god of the Bible. We speak of that god as a being, just for convenience sake, and not from conviction. At bottom, we admit nothing but the mass of contradictory notions between Genesis and Revelation. We attack not a person but a belief, not a being but an idea, not a fact but a fancy.

Lord Brougham long ago pointed out, in his *Life of Voltaire*, that the great French heretic was not guilty of blasphemy, as his enemies alleged; since he had no belief in the actual existence of the god he dissected, analysed, and laughed at. Mr. Ruskin very eloquently defends Byron from the same charge. In *Cain* and elsewhere, the great poet does not impeach God; he merely impeaches the orthodox creed. We may sum up the whole matter briefly. No man satirises the god he believes in, and no man believes in the god he satirises.

We shall not, therefore, be deterred by the cry of "blasphemy!" which is exactly what the Jewish priests shouted against Jesus Christ. If there is a God, he cannot be half such a fool and blackguard as the Bible declares. In destroying the counterfeit we do not harm the reality. And as it is better, in the words of Plutarch, to have no notion of the gods than to have notions which dishonor them, we are satisfied that the Lord (if he exist) will never burn us in hell for denying a few lies told in his name.

The real blasphemers are those who believe in God and blacken his character; who credit him with less knowledge than a child, and less intelligence than an idiot; who make him quibble, deceive, and lie; who represent him as indecent, cruel, and revengeful; who give him the heart of a savage and the brain of a fool. These are the blasphemers.

When the priest steps between husband and wife, with the name of God on his lips, he blasphemes. When, in the name of God, he resists education and science, he blasphemes. When, in the name of God, he opposes freedom of thought and liberty of conscience, he blasphemes. When, in the name of God, he robs, tortures, and kills those who differ from him, he blasphemes. When, in the name of God, he opposes the equal rights of all, he blasphemes. When, in the name of God, he preaches content to the poor and oppressed, flatters the rich and powerful, and makes religious tyranny the handmaiden of political privilege, he blasphemes. And when he takes the Bible in his hand, and says it was written by the inspiration of God, he blasphemes almost beyond forgiveness.

Who are the blasphemers? Not we who preach freedom and progress for all men; but those who try to bind the world with chains of dogma, to burden it, in God's name, with all the foul superstitions of its ignorant past.

CHRISTIANITY AND COMMON SENSE.

There are two things in the world that can never get on together—religion and common sense. Religion deals with the next life, common sense with this; religion points to the sky, common sense to the earth; religion is all imagination, common sense all reason; religion deals with what nobody can understand, common sense with what everybody can understand; religion gives us no return for our investments but flash notes on the bank of expectation, common sense gives us good interest and full security for our capital. They are as opposite as two things can possibly be, and they are always at strife. Religion is always trying to fill the world with delusions, and common sense is always trying to drive them away. Religion says Live for the next world, and common sense says Live for this.

It is in the very nature of things that religion and common sense should hate and oppose each other. They are rivals for the same prize—aspirants to the same throne. In every age a conflict has been going on between them; and although common sense is fast getting the upper hand to-day, the war is far from ended, and we may see some fierce struggles before the combat closes. There can, however, be no doubt as to the issue; for science has appeared on the scene with the most deadly weapons of destruction, and science is the sworn ally of common sense. Nay, is not Science the mighty child of common sense—the fruit of Reason from the lusty embrace of Nature?

Common sense is primitive logic. It does not depend on books, and it is superior to culture. It is the perception of analogy—the instinct of causation. It guides the savage through trackless forests, and the astronomer through infinite space. It makes the burnt child dread the fire, and a Darwin see in a few obvious facts the solution of a mystery. It built the first hut and the last palace; the first canoe and the last ocean steamer. It constructed docks, and laid down railways, applied steam to machinery and locomotion, prompted every mechanical discovery, instigated all material progress, and transformed an ape-like beast into a civilised man.

Even the highest art is full of common sense. Sanity and simplicity are the distinguishing marks of the loftiest genius, which may be described as inspired common sense. The great artist never loses touch of fact; he may let his imagination soar as high as the stars, but he keeps his feet firm-planted on the ground. All the world recognises the sublimity of Greek sculpture and Shakespeare's plays, because they are both true to nature and fact and coincident with everlasting laws. The true sublime is not fantastic; it is solid and satisfying, like a mighty Alp, deep-rooted first of all in the steadfast earth, and then towering up with its vineyards, its pastures, its pine-forests, its glaciers, its precipices, and last of all the silence of infinitude brooding over its eternal snows.

Common sense, the civiliser, has had an especially hard fight with that particular form of religion known as Christianity. When Tertullian said that Christianity was to be believed because it was incredible, he spoke in the true spirit of faith; just as old Sir Thomas Browne did when he found the marvels of religion too weak for his credulity. David Hume expressed the same truth ironically at the conclusion of his *Essay on Miracles*, when he said that it was not reason that persuaded any Christian of the truth of his creed, which was established on the higher ground of faith, and could not be accepted without a miracle.

Common sense is blasphemy. It is the thing which religion dreads most, and which the priests most mortally hate. Common sense dispenses with learned disquisitions, and tries everything with simple mother wit. If, for instance, it hears that a whale swallowed a man, and vomited him up safe and sound three days after, it does not want to know all the physiology of men and whales before deciding if the story is true; it just indulges in a hearty laugh and blows the story to Hades. Miracle-mongers are quite helpless when a man turns round and says, "My dear sir, that story's just a trifle too thin." They see his case is a hopeless one, and leave him to the tender mercies of the Lord of Hosts.

Learning is all very well in its way, but common sense is a great deal better. It is infinitely the best weapon to use against Christianity. Without a knowledge of history, without being acquainted with any science but that of daily life, without a command of Hebrew, Latin and Greek, or any other language than his own, a plain man can take the Bible in his hand and easily satisfy himself it is not the word of God. Common sense tells him not to believe in contradictory statements; common sense tells him that a man could not have found a wife in a land where there were no women; common sense tells him that three millions of people never marched out of any country in one night; common sense tells him that Jesus Christ could not have "gone up" from two places at once; common sense tells him that turning devils out of men

into pigs is a fable not half as good as the poorest of
Æsop's; common sense tells him that nobody but a
skunk would consent to be saved from the penalty of
his own misdeeds by the sufferings of an innocent man;
common sense tells him that while men object to having
their pockets picked and their throats cut, they want
no divine command against theft and murder; common
sense tells him that God never ordered the committal
of such atrocities as those ascribed to him in the Bible;
and common sense tells him that a God of mercy never
made a hell.

Yes, all this is perfectly clear, and the priests know
it. That is why they cry out Blasphemy! every time
they meet it. But that is also precisely the reason
why we should employ it against them. The best
antidote to superstition, the worst enemy of priestcraft, and the best friend of man, is (to parody
Danton's famous formula) Common Sense, and again
Common Sense, and for ever Common Sense.

THE LORD OF LORDS.*

WE are in the midst of a political crisis. The House
of Lords opposes a reform unanimously voted by the
House of Commons. Great demonstrations are being
held all over the country, to insist on the popular will
being carried into effect, and there is a growing cry of
"Down with the Lords." A spectator from another
planet might wonder at all the fuss. He might marvel
how forty millions of people needed to stamp and

---

* Written in August, 1884.

gesticulate against a handful of obstructives. He might imagine that they had only to decree a thing and it would immediately be; that all opposition to their sovereign will would melt away the moment they declared it. This traveller, however, would soon be undeceived. A little study would show him that the people are kept in check by faith and custom. He would learn that the nation is tied down like Gulliver was, by ligatures springing from its own head. Behind the King there is a King of Kings; behind the Lords there is a Lord of Lords. Behind every earthly despotism there is a heavenly one. The rulers of mankind overawe the people by religious terrors. They keep a body of men in their pay, the black army of theology, whose business it is to frighten people from their rights by means of a ghost behind the curtain. Nobody has ever seen the bogie, but we are taught to believe in it from our infancy, and faith supplies the deficiencies of sight. Thus we are enslaved by our own consent. Our will is suborned against our interests. We wear no chains to remind us of our servitude, but our liberty is restrained by the subtle web of superstition, which is so fine as to be imperceptible except to keen and well-practised eyes, and elastic enough to cheat us with a false sense of freedom.

Yes, we must seek in religion the secret of all political tyranny and social injustice. Not only does history show us the bearing of religion on politics—we see it to-day wherever we cast our gaze. Party feeling is so embittered in France because the sharp line of division in politics corresponds with the sharp line of division in religion. On the one side there is Freethought and Republicanism, and on the other Catholicism and Monarchy. Even in England, which at present knows less of the naked despotism of the Catholic Church than any other European country, we are gradually approximating to a similar state of things. Freethought is appearing upon the public stage, and will play its peculiar part as naturally as religion does. Those who fancy that theology and politics have no necessary relations, that you may operate in the one without affecting the other, and that they can and should be kept distinct, are grossly mistaken. Cardinal Newman has well shown how it is the nature of ideas to assimilate to themselves whatever agrees with them, and to destroy whatever disagrees. When once an idea enters the human mind it acts according to the necessary laws of thought. It changes to its own complexion all its mental surroundings, and through every mental and moral channel influences the world of practice outside. The real sovereigns of mankind, who sway its destinies with irresistible power, are not the czars, emperors, kings and lords, nor even the statesmen who enact laws when public sentiment is ripe; they are the great thinkers who mould opinion, the discoverers and enunciators of Truth, the men of genius who pour the leaven of their ideas and enthusiasm into the sluggish brain of humanity.

Even in this crisis it is easy to see how Religion and Freethought are at variance. The Liberal party is not pledged to the abolition of the House of Lords, but the Radical party is. Orthodox Liberalism is Christian, only a little less so than orthodox Conservatism; but Radicalism is very largely sceptical. It would surprise the dullards of both parties to learn how great a portion of the working energy of Radicalism is supplied by Freethinkers. True, many of them are unavowed Freethinkers, yet they are of our party although they do not wear our colors. But setting all these aside, I assert that Radicalism would be immensely weakened by the withdrawal of declared Freethinkers from its ranks. No one in the least acquainted with political organisation would think of disputing this.

Belief in God is the source and principle of all tyranny. This lies in the very nature of things.

For what is God? All definitions of religion from Johnson's down to that of the latest dictionary agree on this one point, that it is concerned with man's relations to *the unknown*. Yes, God is the Unknown, and theology is the science of ignorance. Earl Beaconsfield, in his impish way, once said that where our knowleege ends our religion begins. A truer word was never spoken.

Now the unknown is the terrible. We become fearful the moment we confront the incalculable. Go through the history of religions, consult the various accounts of savage and barbarous faiths at present extant, and you will find that the principle of terror, springing from the unknown, is the essential feature in which they all agree. This terror inevitably begets slavishness. We cannot be cowardly in this respect without its affecting our courage in others. The mental serf is a bodily serf too, and spiritual fetters are the agencies of political thraldom. The man who worships a tyrant in heaven naturally submits his neck to the yoke of tyrants on earth. He who bows his intellect to a priest will yield his manhood to a king. Everywhere on earth we find the same ceremonies attending every form of dependence. The worshipper who now kneels in prayer to God, like the courtier who backs from the presence of the monarch, is performing an apology for the act of prostration which took place alike before the altar and the throne. In both cases it was the adoration of fear, the debasement of the weak before the seat of irresponsible power.

Authority is still the principle of our most refined creeds. The majority of Christians believe in salvation by faith; and what is the God of that dogma but a capricious tyrant, who saves or damns according to his personal whim? The ministers of Protestantism, like the priests of Catholicism, recognise this practically in their efforts to regulate public education. They dare not trust to the effect of persuasion on the unprejudiced mind; they must bias the minds of children by means of dogmatic teaching. They bend the twig in order to warp the tree.

Now God is the supreme principle of authority as he is the essence of the unknown. He is thus the head, front and symbol of terror and slavery, and as such must be assailed by every true soldier of Progress. We shall never enfranchise the world without touching people's superstitions; and even if we abolish the House of Lords we shall still dwell in the house of bondage unless we abolish the Lord of Lords; for the evil principle will remain as a germ to develop into new forms of oppression.

Freethought is the real Savior. When we make a man a Freethinker, we need not trouble greatly about his politics. He is sure to go right in the main. He may mistake here or falter there, but his tendency will always be sound. Thus it is that Freethinkers always vote, work and fight for the popular cause. They have discarded the principle of authority in the heavens above and on the earth beneath, and left it to the Conservative party, to which all religionists belong precisely in proportion to the orthodoxy of their faith. Freethought goes to the root. It reaches the intellect and the conscience, and does not merely work at haphazard on the surface of our material interests and party struggles. It aims at the destruction of all tyranny and injustice by the sure methods of investigation and discussion, and the free play of mind on every subject. It loves Truth and Freedom. It turns away from the false and sterile ideas of the Kingdom of God and faces the true and fruitful idea of the Republic of Man.

CONSECRATING THE COLORS.

THE Queen has recently presented new colors to the first battalion of the Seaforth Highlanders. There was a great parade at Osborne, half the royal family being present to witness her Majesty perform the one piece of business to which she takes kindly in her old age. She has long been, as Lord Beaconsfield said, physically and morally unfit for her many duties; but she is always ready to inspect her troops, to pin a medal or a cross on the breast of that cheap form of valor which excites such admiration in feminine minds, or to thank her brave warriors for exhibiting their heroism on foreign fields against naked savages and half-naked barbarians. The ruling passion holds out strong to the last, and the respectable old lady who is allowed to occupy the English throne because of her harmlessness can still sing, like the Grand Duchess in Offenbach's opera, "Oh, I dote on the military."

But the Queen is not my game. I am "going for" the priests behind her, the mystery-men who give the sanction of religion to all the humbug and hypocrisy, as well as to all the plunder and oppression, that obtain amongst us. Those new colors were consecrated (that is the word) by the Dean of Windsor. The old colors were consecrated forty-two years ago by the Venerable Dr. Vernon Harcourt, Archbishop of York, who was probably a near relative of our pious Home Secretary, the fat member for Derby. If I were a courtier, a sycophant, or an ordinary journalist, I might spend some time in hunting up the actual relationship between these two Harcourts; but being neither, and not caring a straw one way or the other, I content myself, as I shall probably content my readers, with hazarding a conjecture.

Consecrating the colors! What does that mean? First of all it implies the alliance between the soldier and the priest, who are the two arms of tyranny. One holds and the other strikes; one guards and the other attacks; one overawes with terror and delusion, and the other smites with material weapons when the spiritual restraints fail. The black and the red armies are both retainers in the service of Privilege, and they preach or fight exactly as they are bidden. It makes no real difference that the soldier's orders are clear and explicit, while the priest's are mysteriously conveyed through secret channels. They alike obey the mandate of their employers, and take their wages for the work.

In the next place it shows the intimate relation between religion and war. Both belong to the age of faith. When the age of reason has fairly dawned both will be despised and finally forgotten. They are always and everywhere founded on ignorance and stupidity, although they are decorated with all sorts of fine names. The man of sense sees through all these fine disguises. He knows that the most ignorant people are the most credulous, and that the most stupid are the most pugnacious. Educated and thoughtful men shrink alike from the dogmas of religion and the brutalities of war.

Further, this consecration of the colors reminds us that the Christian deity is still the lord of hosts, the god of battles. His eyes delight to look over a purple sea of blood, and his devotees never invoke his name so much as when they are about to emulate his sanguinary characteristics. The Dean of Windsor does not shock, he only gratifies, the feelings of the orthodox world, when he blesses the flag which is to float over scenes of carnage, and flame like a fiend's tongue over the hell of battle, where brothers of the same human family, without a quarrel in the world, but set at variance by thieves and tricksters, maim and mangle and kill each other with fractricidal hands, which ought to have been clasped in friendship and brotherhood.

Yet these hireling priests, who consecrate the banners of war, dare to prate that God is a loving father and that we are all his children. What monstrous absurdity! What disgusting hypocrisy! Surely the parent of mankind, instead of allowing his ministers to mouth his name over the symbols of slaughter, would command them to preach "peace, peace!"

Until the war-drums beat no longer and the battle-flags are furled
In the parliament of man, the federation of the world.

Of course there is a comic side to this, as to almost everything else. The priests of the various nations consecrate rival banners, pray for victory for their own side, and swear that God Almighty is sure to give it them if they trust in him. Now what is the Lord to do when they go on in this way on opposite sides? He is sure to disappoint one party, and he is likely to get devilish little thanks from the other. A wise God would remain neutral, and say, "My comical little fellows, if you will go knocking out each other's brains because they are not strong enough to settle your differences by peaceful means, by all means get through the beastly business as soon as possible; but pray don't trouble me with your petitions for assistance; both sides are fools, and I wash my hands of the whole affair."

I have heard of an old Dutch commander who actually prayed the Lord to remain neutral, although from a different motive. On the eve of battle he addressed the deity in this fashion: "O Lord, we are ten thousand, and they are ten thousand, but we are a darned sight better soldiers than they, and, O Lord, do thou but keep out of it, and we'll give them the soundest thrashing they ever had."

Our Prayer Book pays a very poor compliment to the god of battles. "Give peace in our time, O Lord," says the preacher. "Because there is none other that fighteth for us but only thou O God," responds the congregation. The compilers of the Prayer Book evidently blundered, unless they secretly felt that the

Lord of hosts was used up, and not worth a keg of gunpowder or an old musket.

Consecrating colors, like consecrating graveyards, is after all only a trick of trade. The Dean of Windsor only practises the arts of his profession, and probably laughs in his sleeve at his own public performance. Perhaps he knows that God, as Napoleon said, is on the side of the big battalions; just as, probably, every bishop knows that Church corpses rot exactly like Dissenting corpses, although they lie in consecrated ground. Priestly mummeries will last as long as there is a demand for them. It is of little use to quarrel with the supply. The Freethinker's duty is to lessen the demand.

CHRISTMAS IN HOLLOWAY GAOL.*

THE dullest Christmas I ever spent was in her Majesty's hotel in North London. The place was spacious, but not commodious; it was magnificent in the mass, but very petty in detail; it was designed with extreme care for the safety of its many guests, but with a complete disregard of their comfort; and it soon palled upon the taste, despite the unremitting attentions of a host of liveried servants. How I longed for a change of scene, if what I constantly gazed upon may be so described; but I was like a knight in some enchanted castle, surrounded with attendants, yet not at liberty to walk out. The hospitality of my residence, however, was by no

---

* I was imprisoned there for "blasphemy" from February 1883 to February 1884, by sentence of a Roman Catholic judge, Mr. Justice North.

means sumptuous. The table did not groan beneath a weight of viands, or gleam with glowing wines. Its poverty was such that a red-herring would have been a glorious treat, and a dose of physic an agreeable variety. Why then, you may ask, did I not quit this inhospitable hotel, and put up at another establishment? Because I was invited by her Majesty, and her Majesty's invitations are commands.

Speaking by the card, Christmas-day in Holloway was treated as a Sunday. There was no work and no play then, the dinner was the poorest and worst cooked in the whole week, and the only diversion was a morning or afternoon visit to chapel, where we had the satisfaction of learning that heaven was an eternal Sunday.

The fibre put into my cell to be picked by my industrious fingers had all been removed the previous evening, lest I should desecrate the sacred day by pursuing my ordinary avocation. My apartment was therefore clean and tidy, and by the aid of a bit of dubbin I managed to give an air of newness to my well-worn shoes. The attendants had, however, omitted to provide me with a Sunday suit, so I was obliged to don my working clothes, in which graceless costume I had to perform my religious devotions in the house of God, where an ill-dressed person is always regarded as an exceptionally bad sinner, and expected to show an extraordinary amount of humility and contrition. Linen was never a burning question in Holloway Hotel, and cuffs and collars were unknown, except when a short guest wore a long shirt. My toilet was therefore easily completed; and with a good wash, and the energetic use of a three-inch comb, I was soon ready for the festivities of the season.

At eight o'clock I received the first instalment of my Christmas fare, in the shape of three-quarters of a pint of tea and eight ounces of dry bread. Whether the price of groceries was affected by the Christmas demand, or whether the kitchen was demoralised by the holiday, I am unable to decide ; but I noticed that the decoction was more innocuous than usual, although I had thought its customary strength could not be weakened without a miracle. My breakfast being devised on the plainest vegetarian principles, there was no occasion for grace before meat, so I sipped the tea and munched the bread (eight ounces straight off requires a great deal of mastication) without breathing a word of thanks to the giver of all good things.

After a remarkably short hour's tramp round the exercise ring in a thieves' procession, doing the rogue's march without the music, I returned to my cell, and sitting down on my little three-legged stool, I was soon lost in thought. I wondered what my wife was doing, how she was spending the auspicious day. What a "merry Christmas" for a woman with her husband eating his heart out in gaol! But "that way madness lies," and I had fought down the demon too long to give way then. Springing to my feet, I sped up and down my cell like a caged animal, and after many maledictions on "the accursed creed," I succeeded in stilling the tumult of my emotions. A great calm followed this storm, and resuming my seat and leaning my back against the plank-bed, I took a scornful retrospect of my prosecution and trial. How insignificant looked the Tylers, Giffards, Norths and Harcourts! How noble the friends and the party who had stood by me in the dark hour of defeat! A few short weeks, and I should be free again to join their ranks and strike hard in the thickest of the battle, under the grand old flag of Freethought.

The chapel-bell roused me from phantasy. The other half of the prison disgorged its inmates, and I could hear the sound of their tramping to the sanctuary. While they were engaged there I read a chapter of Gibbon; after which I heard the "miserable sinners" return from the chapel to their cells.

At twelve o'clock came my second instalment of Christmas fare : six ounces of potatoes, eight ounces of bread and a mutton chop. Being on hospital diet, I had this trinity for my dinner every day for nine months, and words cannot describe the nauseous monotony of the *menu*. The other prisoners had the regular Sunday's diet: bread, potatoes and suet-pudding. After dinner I went for another short hour's tramp in the yard. The officers seemed to relax their usual rigor, and many of the prisoners exchanged greetings. " How did yer like the figgy duff ?" " Did the beef stick in yer stomach ?" Such were the flowers of conversation that afternoon. From the talk around me, I gathered that under the old management, before the Government took over the prison, all the inmates had a " blow out " on Christmas-day, consisting of beef, vegetables, plum-pudding and a pint of beer. Some of the " old hands " bitterly bewailed the decadence in prison hospitality. Their lamentations were worthy of a Conservative orator at a rural meeting. The present was a poor thing compared with the past, and they sighed for " the tender grace of a day that is dead."

After exercise I went to chapel. The schoolmaster, who was a very pleasant gentleman, had drilled the singing class into a fair state of efficiency, and they sang one or two Christmas hymns in pretty good style ; but the effect of their efforts was considerably marred by the rest of the congregation, whose unmusical voices, bad sense of time, and ignorance of the tune, more than once nearly brought the performance to an untimely end. Parson Playford followed with a seasonable sermon, which would have been more heartily relished on a fuller stomach. He told us what a blessed time Christmas was, and how people did well to be joyous on the anniversary of their Savior's birth ; after which I presume he returned to the bosom of his family, and celebrated the birth of Christ with liberal doses of turkey, goose, beef, pudding, and communion wine. Before dismissing us with his blessing to our " little rooms," which was his habitual euphemism for our cells, he said that he could not wish us a happy Christmas in our unhappy condition, but would wish us a peaceful Christmas; and he ventured to promise us that boon, if after leaving chapel, we fell on our knees, and besought pardon for our sins. Most of the prisoners received this advice with a grin, for their cell-floors were black-leaded, and practising genuflexions in their "little-rooms" gave too much knee-cap to their trousers.

At six o'clock I had my third instalment of Christmas fare, consisting of another eight ounces of bread and three quarters of a pint of tea. The last mouthfuls were consumed to the accompaniment of church bells. The neighboring gospel-shops were announcing their evening performance, and the sound penetrated into my cell through the open ventilator. The true believers were wending their way to God's house, and the heretic, who had dared to deride their creed and denounce their hypocrisy, was regaling himself on dry bread and warm water in one of their prison-cells. And the bells rang out against each other from the many steeples with a wild glee as I paced up and down my narrow dungeon. They seemed mad with the intoxication of victory; they mocked me with their bacchanalian frenzy of triumph. But I smiled grimly, for their clamor was no more than the ancient fool's-shout, "Great is Diana of the Ephesians." Great Christ has had his day since, but he in turn is dead; dead in man's intellect, dead in man's heart, dead in man's life; a mere phantom, flitting about the aisles of churches where priestly mummers go through the rites of a phantom creed.

I took my Bible and read the story of Christ's birth in Matthew and Luke. What an incongruous jumble of absurdities! A poor fairy tale of the world's childhood, utterly insignificant beside the stupendous wonders which science has revealed to its manhood. From the fanciful little story of the Magi following a star, to Shelley's "Worlds on worlds are rolling ever," what an advance! As I retired to sleep upon my plank-bed my mind was full of these reflections. And when the gas was turned out, and I was left alone in darkness and silence, I felt serene and almost happy.

WHO KILLED CHRIST?

WITHOUT committing ourselves to a full acceptance of the Gospel story of Christ's death, with all its monstrous miracles and absurd defiance of Roman and Jewish legal procedure, we propose to take the story as it stands for the purpose of discussing the question at the top of this article.

The ordinary Christian will exclaim that Jesus was murdered by those infernal Jews. Ever since they had the power of persecuting the Jews—that is, ever since the days of Constantine—the Christians have acted on the assumption that the countrymen of Jesus did actually cry out before Pilate, "His blood be on our heads!" and that they and their posterity deserved any amount of robbery and outrage until they unanimously confessed their sin and worshipped him whom they crucified. It made no difference that the contemporaries of Jesus Christ could not transmit their guilt to their offspring. The Christians continued, century after century, to act in the spirit of the sailor in the story. Coming ashore after a long voyage, Jack attended church and heard a pathetic sermon on the Crucifixion. On the following day he looked into the window of a print-shop, and saw a picture of Jesus on the cross. Just then a Jew came and looked into the window; whereupon the sailor, pointing to the picture, asked the Hebrew gentleman whether he recognised it. "That's Jesus," said the Jew, and the sailor immediately knocked him down. Surprised at this treatment, the Hebrew gentleman inquired the reason. "Why," said the sailor, "didn't you infernal Jews crucify him?" The poor son of Abraham admitted the fact, but explained that it happened nearly two thousand years ago. "No matter," said the sailor, "I only heard of it yesterday."

Now it is perfectly clear, according to the Gospels, that the Jews did *not* kill Jesus. Unless they lynched him they had no power to put him to death. Judæa was then a Roman province, and in every part of the Empire the extreme penalty of the law was only inflicted by the Roman governor. Nevertheless it may be argued that the Jews *really* killed him, although they did not actually shed his blood, as they clamored for his death and terrorised Pontius Pilate into ordering a judicial murder. But suppose we take this view of the case: does it therefore follow that they acted without justification? Was not Jesus, in their judgment, guilty of blasphemy, and was not that a deadly crime under the Mosaic law? "He that blasphemeth the name of the Lord," says Leviticus xxiv. 16, "shall surely be put to death." Were not the Jews, then, carrying out the plain commandment of Jehovah?

Nor was this their only justification. In another part of the Mosaic law (Deut. xiii. 6-10), the Jews were ordered to kill anyone, whether mother, son, daughter, husband, or wife, who should entice them to worship other gods. Now it is expressly maintained by the overwhelming majority of divines that Jesus asserted his own godhead. He is reported as saying, "I and my father are one," and, as St. Paul says, "He thought it no robbery to be equal to God." Were not the Jews, then, bound to kill him if they could?

Let it not be supposed that *we* would have killed him. We are not excusing the Jews as men, but as observers of the Mosaic law and worshippers of Jehovah. Their God is responsible for the death of Jesus, and if Jesus was a portion of that very deity, he was responsible for his own death. His worshippers had learnt the lesson so well that they killed their own God when he came in disguise.

It is contended by some Christians that Pontius Pilate killed Jesus. According to these arguers, Pilate knew that Jesus was innocent, and the execution was therefore a murder. But is it not perfectly obvious from the Gospel story that Pilate tried to save Jesus? Did not the obstinate prisoner plead guilty to what was really a charge of sedition? Did he attempt any defence? Did he call any witnesses? Was he not contumacious? And had Pilate any alternative to sentencing him to the legal punishment of his crime?

Other friends of Jesus lay the blame of his death on Judas Iscariot. But the whole story of his "betrayal" of Jesus is a dowright absurdity. How could he *sell* his master when the commodity was common? What sense is there in his being paid to indicate the best-known man in Jerusalem? Even if the story were true, it appears that Jesus knew what Judas was doing, and as he could easily have returned to Galilee, he was accessory to his own fate. It may also be pointed out that Judas only killed Jesus if the tragedy would not have occurred without him; in which case he was the proximate cause of the Crucifixion, and consequently a benefactor to all who are saved by the blood of Christ. Instead of execration, therefore, he deserves praise, and even the statue which Disraeli suggested as his proper reward.

Who killed Christ? Why himself. His brain gave way. He was demented. His conduct at Jerusalem was that of a maniac. His very language showed a loss of balance. Whipping the dove-sellers and money-changers, not out of the Temple, but out of its unsanctified precincts, was lunatic violence. Those merchants were fulfilling a necessary, reputable function; selling doves to women who required them as burnt offerings, and exchanging the current Roman money for the sacred Jewish coins which alone were accepted by the Temple priests. It is easy to call them thieves, but they were not tried, and their evidence is unheard. If they cheated, they must have been remarkably clever, for all their customers were Jews. Besides, there were proper tribunals for the correction of such offences, and no one who was not beside himself would think of going into a market and indiscriminately whipping the traders and dashing down their stalls. Certainly any man who did it now would be arrested, if he were not lynched on the spot, and would either be imprisoned or detained at Her Majesty's pleasure.

Quite in keeping with these displays of temper was the conduct of Jesus before Pilate. A modicum of common sense would have saved him. He was not required to tell a lie or renounce a conviction. All that was necessary to his release was to plead not guilty and defend himself against the charge of sedition. His death, therefore, was rather a suicide than a martyrdom. Unfortunately the jurisprudence of that age was less scientific than the one which now prevails; the finer differences between sanity and insanity were not discriminated; otherwise Jesus would have been remanded for inquiries into his mental condition.

As a man Jesus died because he had not the sense to live. As a God he must have died voluntarily. In either case it is an idle, gratuitous, enervating indulgence in "the luxury of woe" to be always afflicting ourselves with the story of his doom. Great and good men have suffered and died since, and other lessons are needed than any that may be learnt at the foot of the Cross.

DID JESUS ASCEND?

THE story of the Ascension of Jesus Christ is as absurd as the story of his Resurrection. Both, in fact, are the products of an age prone to believe in the wonderful. So prevalent was the popular belief in the supernatural character of great men, that the comparatively cultivated Romans accepted a monstrous fable about Julius Cæsar. "The enthusiasm of the multitude," says Mr. Froude, "refused to believe that he was dead. He was supposed to have ascended into heaven, not in adulatory metaphor, but in literal and prosaic fact."

Similarly the enthusiasm of the first followers of Jesus, and especially of hysterical ladies like Mary Magdalene, refused to believe that *he* was dead. The fable of his resurrection was gradually developed, and his ascension was devised to round off the story. Whoever will read St. Paul's epistles first, and the Gospels and the Acts afterwards, will see how the Christ myth grew from vagueness to precision under the shaping imagination of the Church of the first century after the age of the Apostles.

It is a significant fact that the appearances of Jesus after his Resurrection were all made to the faithful, and his ascension took place before them, without a single impartial person being allowed to witness an event of which it was of the utmost importance for the world to have positive assurance.

When we turn to the Gospels and the Acts, five documents whose authorship is absolutely unknown, we find the most contradictory accounts of what happened after the Resurrection. It may safely be affirmed that five such witnesses would damn any case in a legal court where the laws of evidence are respected.

These witnesses cannot even agree as to whether the risen Jesus was a man or a ghost. Now he comes through a closed door, and anon he eats broiled fish and honeycomb; now he vanishes, after walking and talking with his disciples, and anon he allows the sceptical Thomas to examine the wounds of his crucifixion as a proof that he was not a spirit, but solid flesh and blood.

According to Matthew's account, Jesus first appeared to the women—as is very probable! Mark says his first appearance was to Mary Magdalene alone; Luke says it was two of the disciples on the road to Emmaus.

His subsequent appearances are recorded with the same harmony. While Matthew makes him appear but once, Mark makes him appear three times—to the women, to the two disciples going to Emmaus, and to the eleven apostles. Luke makes him appear but twice, and John four times—to Mary Magdalene alone, to the disciples in a room without Thomas, to the same again with Thomas, and to the same once more at Tiberias. John is the only one who tells the pretty story about Thomas, and John of course is the only one who mentions the spear-thrust in Christ's side at the crucifixion, because he wanted a hole for Thomas to put his hand into, and the other evangelists had no need of such a provision.

Matthew and Mark relate that the disciples were told by an angel to go to Galilee, while Luke keeps them in the Holy City, and Acts declares that Jesus expressly "commanded them that they should not depart from Jerusalem."

The ascension itself, which involved the last appearance of Jesus, as well as his disappearance, is not related by Matthew, nor is it related by John. Now Matthew and John are *supposed* to have been apostles. If the ascension happened they must have witnessed it; but both of them are silent, and the story of the ascension comes from three writers who were *not present*.

Nor do these three writers agree with each other. Luke informs us that Jesus ascended from Bethany, a short distance from Jerusalem, on the very day of the Resurrection, or at the latest the next morning; while Mark, without any precision as to time, distinctly affirms that Jesus ascended from Galilee, which was at least sixty miles from Jerusalem. Now the ascension could not have occurred at two different places, and, in the absence of corroborative testimony, Mark and Luke destroy each other as witnesses.

The author of Acts agrees with Mark as to the place, but differs both from Mark and Luke as to the time. He declares that Jesus spent forty days (off and on) with his disciples before levitating. This constitutes another difficulty. Mark, Luke, and the author of Acts must all leave the court in disgrace, for it is too late for them to patch up a more harmonious story.

According to the detailed account in Acts, Jesus ascended in the presence of his apostles, including Matthew and John, who appear to have mistrusted their eyesight. After making a speech he was "taken up, and a cloud received him out of their sight." He was in a cloud, and they were in a cloud, and the millions who believe them are in a cloud.

The time of the year is seasonable for an examination of the story of the Ascension. Would that the opportunity were taken by Christians, who believe what they have been taught with scarcely a moment's investigation, and read the Bible as lazily as they smoke their pipes. We do not ask them to take our word for anything. Let them examine for themselves. If they will do this, we have no fear as to the result. A belief in the New Testament story of the supernatural Christ is impossible to any man who candidly sifts and honestly weighs the evidence.

If Christians would pursue their investigations still further they would soon satisfy themselves that the life, death, resurrection, and ascension of Jesus Christ are largely, if not entirely, mythical. Now, for instance, when they are preparing to celebrate the ascension of Christ, they are welcoming the ascension of the Sun. The great luminary is (apparently) rising higher and higher in the heaven, shedding his warmer beams on the earth, and gladdening the hearts of man. And there is more connection between the Son and the Sun than ordinary Christians imagine.

THE RISING SON.

You are requested to read the above title carefully. Notice the spelling of the last word. It is *son*, not *sun*. The difference to the eye is only in one letter. The substantial difference is very great. Yet in the end the distinction between the Son and the Sun vanishes. Originally they were one and the same thing, and they will be so again when Christianity is properly understood.

Supposing that Jesus of Nazareth ever lived, it is impossible to know, with any approach to accuracy, what he really was. With the exception of four epistles by Saint Paul—in which we find a highly mystical Christ, and not a portrait or even a sketch of an actual man—we have no materials for a biography of Jesus written within a hundred years of his death. Undoubtedly *some* documents existed before the Canonical and Apocryphal Gospels, but they were lost through neglect or suppression, and what we have is simply the concoction of older materials by an unscrupulous Church.

During the interval between the real or supposed death of Jesus and the date of the gospels, there was plenty of time for the accumulation of any quantity of mythology. The east was full of such material, only waiting, after the destruction of the old national religions under the sway of Rome, to be woven into the texture of a non-national system as wide as the limits of the Empire.

Protestants are able to recognise a vast deal of Paganism in the teaching and ritual of the Roman Catholic Church. On that side they keep an open eye. On the other side their eye is shut. If they opened it they would see plenty of Paganism in the gospels.

The only fixed date in the career of Jesus is his birthday. This is known by every scholar to be fictitious. The primitive Church was ignorant of the day on which Jesus was born. But what was unknown to the apostles, one of whom is said to have been his very brother, was opportunely discovered by the Church three hundred years afterwards. For some time the nativity of Jesus had been celebrated on all sorts of days, but the Church brought about uniformity by establishing the twenty-fifth of December. This was the Pagan festival of the nativity of the Sun. The Church simply appropriated it, in order to bring over the Pagan population by a change of doctrine without a change of rites and customs.

It may be objected that the primitive Church did not inquire as to the birthday of Jesus until it was too late to ascertain it. But this objection cannot possibly apply to the resurrection, the date of which is involved in equal uncertainty, although one would expect it to be precisely known and regularly commemorated. For many ages the celebration was irregular. Different Sundays were kept, and sometimes other days, in various weeks of March and April. Finally, after fierce disputes and excommunications, the present system was imposed upon the whole Catholic world.

Easter is, in fact, decided astronomically, by a process in which sun-worship and moon-worship are both conciliated. The starting point is the vernal equinox, which was the time of a common Pagan festival. The very name of Easter is of heathen origin. All its customs are bequeathed to us from far-off Pagan ancestors. Easter eggs, symbolising the life of the universe, have been traced back to the Romans, Greeks, Persians, and Egyptians.

When the Christians celebrate the resurrection of Christ they are imitating the ancient "heathen," who at the same time of the year commemorated the resurrection of the Sun, and his manifest triumph over the powers of darkness. And when the moderns prepare to celebrate the ascension of Christ, they are really welcoming the ascension of the Sun. The great luminary—father of light and lord of life—is then (apparently) rising higher and higher in heaven, shedding his warmer beams on the earth, and gladdening the hearts of men.

Churches and altars are decked with vegetation, which is another relic of nature-worship. Life is once more bursting forth under the kindling rays of the sun. Hope springs afresh in the heart of man. His fancy sees the pastures covered with flocks and herds, the corn waving in the breeze, and the grapes plumping in the golden sunshine, big with the blood of earth and the fire of heaven.

According to the Apostles' Creed, Jesus descended into hell between his death and resurrection. That is also a relic of sun-worship. During the dark, cold winter the sun descended into the underworld, which is the real meaning of Hades. Misunderstanding this circumstance, or deliberately perverting it, the early Church fabricated the monstrous fable that Jesus "preached unto the spirits in prison," as we read in the first epistle of Peter. One of the apocryphal gospels gives a lively account of how he harried the realm of Old Harry, emptying the place wholesale, and robbing the poor Devil of all his illustrious subjects, from Adam to John the Baptist.

A volume might be filled with illustrations of the mythology of the Resurrection. Our present space is limited, and we must let the above suffice. Anyone who reads the gospel story of the resurrection and ascension of Jesus Christ, with a careful eye and a critical mind, will see that it is not historical. Such witnesses, so loose in statement and so contradictory of each other, would collapse in a few minutes in any court of law. They do not write as spectators, and they were not spectators. What they give us is the legendary and mythical story that had taken possession of the Christian mind long after all the contemporaries of Jesus were dead.

Our belief, in conclusion, is that the Rising Sun will outlast the Rising Son. The latter is gradually, but very surely, perishing. Even professed Christians are giving up the miraculous elements of the gospels. But who would give up the Sun, which has warmed, lighted, and fertilised the earth for millions of years, and will do so for millions of years after the death of Christianity?

ST. PAUL'S VERACITY.

A VERY pretty storm has been raised (and settled) by the *Independent* and *Nonconformist*. It raged around the Apostle Paul and Mr. Herbert Spencer, who both come out of it apparently not a penny the worse. Mr. Spencer has a chapter on Veracity in his recently published *Principles of Ethics*, wherein he cites Paul as a violator of this virtue, and remarks that "apparently piquing himself on his craft and guile," he "elsewhere defends his acts by contending that 'the truth of God hath more abounded through my lie unto his glory.'" This roused the ire of the *Independent*, and Mr. Spencer was informed that his extraordinary aspersion on the Apostle's character was wholly without justification. Whereupon the great Evolutionist replied that two days before receiving the *Independent* he had "sent to the printer the copy of a cancel to be substituted for the page in which there occurs the error you point out." Mr. Spencer goes on to say that he had trusted to assistants, and been misled on this particular point as on a few others.

"The inductions contained in the *Principles of Sociology* and in Part II. of the *Principles of Ethics* are based mainly, though not wholly, upon the classified materials contained in *The Descriptive Sociology*, compiled between 1867 and 1881 by three University men I engaged for the purpose. When using this compilation of facts concerning sixty-eight different societies I have habitually trusted to the compilers. For even had I been in good health, it would have been impossible for me to verify all their extracts from multitudinous books. In some cases, where the work was at hand, I have referred for verification; and have usually done so in the case of extracts from the Bible; now and then, as I remember, rejecting the extracts given to me as being not justified by the context. But in the case in point it seems that I had not been sufficiently careful. It is only after reading the preceding chapter that it becomes clear that the passage I quoted must be taken as part of an argument with an imaginary interlocutor, rather than as expressive of St. Paul's own sentiment. It must, I think, be admitted that the presentation of the thought is a good deal complicated, and, in the absence of the light thrown upon it by the preceding chapter, is liable to be misunderstood. I regret that I misunderstood it."

This explanation and apology are, of course, most satisfactory. Saint Paul is cleared by Mr. Spencer's certificate, and the *Independent* remarks that this is "a noble codicil to Mr. Spencer's chapter on Veracity." Nay, it professes high "admiration" for him as the "greatest living philosopher of the English-speaking race." Thus the "Comedy of Errors" is followed by

"All's Well that Ends Well," and the curtain falls on compliments and embraces.

It really seems a shame to disturb this pleasant harmony, but we feel compelled to say something to the *Independent* and to Mr. Herbert Spencer about the Apostle Paul.

In the first place we must observe that Mr. Spencer's "erroneous" statement about the great apostle, while it may be an *aspersion*, is certainly not *extraordinary*. It has repeatedly been made by the apostle's adverse critics, and even by some of his admirers. Without citing a long list of them, we will give two—both English, and both judicial. Jeremy Bentham, the great reformer of our jurisprudence, wrote a work entitled *Not Paul, but Jesus*, in which he contends through four hundred pages that Paul was mercenary, ambitious, and an unscrupulous liar. To cull a single passage from Bentham's book is like picking one raisin from a rich plum-pudding. Every sentence is an indictment. And surely after Bentham's trenchant performance it is idle for an English journal to pretend that there is anything "extraordinary" in Mr. Spencer's "erroneous" accusation. The other judicial writer, also belonging to the English race, is Sir Richard David Hanson, who was for some time Chief Justice of South Australia. In his able work on *The Apostle Paul* there is an admirable summing-up of the hero's character. After admitting Paul's ability, persistence, courage, and other virtues, he remarks—"But these are accompanied by what in an uninspired man would be called pride, jealousy, disdain, invective, sophistry, time-serving and intolerance." This is pretty strong; and "sophistry" and "time-serving" are only euphemisms for *lying* in preaching and practice.

So much for the *Independent*, and now for Mr. Spencer. It must be observed that one part of his "erroneous" statement *cannot* be repudiated. The apostle distinctly says, "being crafty, I caught you with guile" (2 Cor. xii. 16), so that "piquing himself on his craft and guile" must stand while this text remains in the Epistle. Mr. Spencer allows that, in the third of Romans, the "presentation of the thought is a good deal complicated," and "liable to be misunderstood"; but, if read in the light of the preceding chapter, the passage about lying to the glory of God "must be taken as part of an argument with an imaginary interlocutor." Perhaps so; but *which* is speaking in the seventh verse? Paul or his opponent? Mr. Spencer does not say. Yet this is the real point. To us it seems that *Paul* is speaking. Of course it may be urged that he is speaking ironically. But this is not Mr. Spencer's contention. It is not clear what he *does* mean; in fact, he seems to have caught a little of Paul's confusion.

We have no objection to reading the seventh verse of the third of Romans in the light of the preceding chapter. But should it not also be read in the light of Christian history? Have honest openness and strict veracity been *ever* regarded as essential virtues in the propagation of the gospel? And why is it likely that Paul, of all men, escaped the contagion of fraud, which has always disgraced the Christian Church? The ordinary Protestant imagines, or pretends, that the Catholic Church has been the great impostor; but this is nonsense to the student of early Christianity. Mosheim remarks that the "pernicious maxim" that "those who make it their business to deceive with a view of promoting the cause of truth were deserving rather of commendation than of censure," was "*very early* recognised by the Christians." Bishop Ellicott similarly observes that "history forces upon us the recognition of pious fraud as a principle which was by no means inoperative in the *earliest ages* of Christianity." Middleton likewise reflects that the bold defiance of honesty and truth displayed by the Fathers of the fourth century "could not have been acquired, or become general at once, but must have been carried gradually to that height, by custom and the example of former times, and a long experience of what the credulity and superstition of the multitude would bear." So far, indeed, were the "*earlier ages*" from being remarkable for integrity, that Middleton says there never was "any period of time" in which fraud and forgery more abounded. The learned Casaubon also complains that it was in "the *earliest times* of the Church" that it was "considered a capital exploit to lend to heavenly truth the help of invention, in order that the new doctrine might be more readily allowed by the wise among the Gentiles." Mosheim even finds that the period of fraud began "not long after Christ's ascension." And it continued, without a blush of shame on Christian cheeks; not growing worse, for that was impossible; until Eusebius, in the fourth century, remarked as a matter of course that he had written what redounded to the glory, and suppressed whatever tended to the disgrace of religion.

Now if fraud was practised as a pious principle in the very earliest ages of Christianity; if it continued for as many centuries as it could pass with impunity; if it was so systematic and prolonged, and carried to such a height, that Herder declared "Christian veracity" fit to rank with "Punic Faith"; what right has anyone —even a Christian editor—to place Paul above suspicion, or to find a "monstrous" blunder in his being accused of lying, especially when the historic practice of his co-religionists seems to many persons to be more than half countenanced by his own language?

We are not concerned to *press* the charge of lying against St. Paul. There have been so many liars in the Christian Church that one more or less makes very little difference. On the other hand, we cannot accept Mr. Spencer's certificate without reservation. He admits that Paul's language is obscure; and perhaps a little obscurity is to be expected when a man is replying to an accusation which he is not wholly able to rebut.

NO FAITH WITH HERETICS.

During the Crusades, when the Christians were wantonly fighting against their superiors in civilisation and humanity, the doctrine was promulgated and obeyed that no faith should be kept with infidels, and this was subsequently put in force against heretics. Thousands of Mohammedan prisoners were butchered in cold blood, although their safety had been confirmed by an oath; and this infamous practice was afterwards pursued with respect to the "heretical" sects when the Papal troops desolated some of tht fairest parts of Europe. Not only was there no salvation outside the Church, but even the ordinary laws of human society were held to be abrogated. This wickedness, perhaps, reached its culmination in the Spanish conquest of America. Few Christians were civilised enough to condemn these purjured banditti, but Montaigne in France, and Raleigh in England, were glorious exceptions, and both of them were under a just suspicion of heterodoxy.

Protestants as well as Catholics were infected with this infamous bigotry. Luther himself was not free from taint, and Calvin's treachery against Servetus is an eternal blot on his character.

"No faith with heretics" took a new form when the downright violation of an oath became too dissonant to the spirit of an improved civilisation. It found expression in robbing the heretic of political and social rights, and above all in treating him as outside the pale of honor. Slandering him was no libel. Every bigot claimed the right to say anything against his character, for the purpose of bringing his opinions into hatred and contempt. All the dictates of charity were cast aside; his good actions were misrepresented, and his failings maliciously exaggerated. If Voltaire spent

J

thousands in charity, he did it for notoriety; if he wrote odes to beautiful or accomplished ladies, he was a wretched debauchee. If Thomas Paine made sacrifices for liberty, he did it because he had a private grudge against authority; if he befriended the wife and family of a distressed Republican, he only sought to gratify his lust; if he spent a convivial hour with a friend, he was an inveterate drunkard; and if he contracted a malignant abscess by lying for months in a damp, unwholesome dungeon, his sufferings were the nemesis of a wicked, profligate life.

An English precursor of Voltaire and Paine wrote *A Discourse on Freethinking*. His name was Anthony Collins, and in a certain sense he was the father of English Freethought. He was a man of exemplary life and manners, yet the saintly Bishop Berkeley said he " deserved to be denied the common benefit of air and water." One of Collins's antagonists was the famous Dr. Bentley; and although Collins was a man of fortune, the ridiculous calumny was started that he sought and obtained Bentley's aasistance in adversity. The author of this calumny was Richard Cumberland, a grandson of Bentley, and in other respects an estimable man. His mistake was pointed out by Isaac D'Israeli, who told him the person he meant was *Arthur* Collins, the historical compiler. But Cumberland perpetuated the calumny, remarking that " it should stand, because it could do no harm to any but to Anthony Collins, whom he considered little short of an Atheist."

Another story about Collins, which has frequently done duty in Christian publications, is that a visitor found him reading the New Testament, and that he remarked, " I have but one book, but that is the best." Fortunately I am able to give the origin of this story. It is told of *William* Collins, the poet, by Dr. Johnson, and may be found in the second volume (p. 239) of that writer's " Miscellaneous and Fugitive Pieces," published by Davies in Johnson's lifetime. It was not Anthony Collins, therefore; but what does that matter? It was a gentleman named *Collins*; his other name is indifferent. Besides, the story is so much more affecting when told of *Anthony*.

Look at the lying stories of infidel death-beds; glance at the scurrilities of an outcast minister which are gratuitously circulated by the enemies of Colonel Ingersoll; observe on how many platforms Mr. Bradlaugh has pulled out his watch and given the Almighty five minutes to strike him dead; listen to the grotesque libels on every leading Freethinker which are solemnly circulated by Christian malice; and you will behold the last fruit of a very old tree, which is slowly but surely perishing. It once bore scaffolds, stakes, prisons and torture rooms; it now bears but libels and insinuations.

THE LOGIC OF PERSECUTION.

NEITHER the cruelty of tyrants, nor the ambition of conquerors, has wrought so much mischief and suffering as the principle of persecution. The crimes of a Nero, the ravages of an Attila, afflict the world for a season, and then cease and are forgotten, or only linger in the memory of history. But persecution operates incessantly like a natural force. With the universality of light, it radiates in every direction. The palace is not too proud for its entrance, nor is the cottage too humble. It affects every relationship of life. Its action is exhibited in public through imprisonment, torture, and bloodshed, and in private through the tears of misery and the groans of despair.

But worse remains. Bodies starve and hearts break, but at last there comes "the poppied sleep, the end of all." Grief is buried in the grave, Nature covers it with a mantle of grass and flowers, and the feet of joy trip merrily over the paths once trodden by heavy-footed care. Yet the more subtle effects of persecution remain with the living. *They are not screwed down in the coffin and buried with the dead.* They become part of the pestilential atmosphere of cowardice and hypocrisy which saps the intellectual manhood of society, so that bright-eyed inquiry sinks into blear-eyed faith, and the rich vitality of active honest thought falls into the decrepitude of timid and slothful acquiescence.

What is this principle of persecution, and how is it generated and developed in the human mind? Now that it is falling into discredit, there is a tendency on the part of Christian apologists to ascribe it to our natural hatred of contradiction. Men argue and quarrel, and if intellectual differences excite hostility in an age like this, how easy it was for them to excite the bitterest animosity in more ignorant and barbarous ages! Such is the plea now frequently advanced. No doubt it wears a certain plausibility, but a little investigation will show its fallacy. Men and women are so various in their minds, characters, circumstances, and interests, that if left to themselves they inevitably form a multiplicity of ever-shifting parties, sects, fashions and opinions; and while each might resent the impertinence of disagreement from its own standard, the very multiformity of the whole mass must preserve a general balance of fair play, since every single sect with an itch for persecuting would be confronted by an overwhelming majority of dissidents. It is obvious, therefore, that persecution can only be indulged in when some particular form of opinion is in the ascendant: and if this form is artificially developed; if it is the result, not of knowledge and reflection, but of custom and training; if, in short, it is rather a superstition than a belief; you have a condition of things highly favorable to the forcible suppression of heresy. Now, throughout history, there is one great form of opinion which *has been* artificially developed, which has been accepted through faith and not through study, which has always been concerned with alleged occurrences in the remote past or the inaccessible future, and which has also been systematically maintained in its "pristine purity" by an army of teachers who have pledged themselves to inculcate the ancient faith without any admixture of their own intelligence.

That form of opinion is Religion. Accordingly we should expect to find its career always attended with persecution, and the expectation is amply justified by a cursory glance at the history of every faith. There is, indeed, one great exception; but, to use a popular though inaccurate phrase, it is an exception which proves the rule. Buddhism has never persecuted. But Buddhism is rather a philosophy than a religion; or, if a religion, it is not a theology, and that is the sense attached to *religion* in this article.

All such religions have persecuted, do persecute, and will persecute while they exist. Let it not be supposed, however, that they punish heretics on the open ground that the majority must be right and the minority must be wrong, or that some people have a right to think while others have only the right to acquiesce. No, that is too shameless an avowal; nor would it, indeed, be the real truth. There is a principle in religions which has always been the sanction of persecution, and if it be true, persecution is more than right, it is a duty. That principle is Salvation by Faith.

If a certain belief is necessary to salvation, if to reject it is to merit damnation, and to undermine it is to imperil the eternal welfare of others, there is only one course open to its adherents; they must treat the heretic as they would treat a viper. He is a poisonous creature to be swiftly extinguished.

But not *too* swiftly, for he has a soul that may still be saved. Accordingly he is sequestered to prevent further harm, an effort is made to convert him, then he is punished, and the rest is left with God. That his conversion is attempted by torture, either physical or mental, is not an absurdity; it is consonant to the doctrine of salvation by faith. For if God punishes or rewards us according to our possession or lack of faith, it follows that faith is within the power of will. Accordingly the heretic, to use Dr. Martineau's expression, is reminded not of arguments but of motives, not of evidence but of fear, not of proofs but of perils, not of reasons but of ruin. When we recognise that the understanding acts independently of volition, and that the threat of punishment, while it may produce silence or hypocrisy, *cannot* alter belief, this method of procedure strikes us as a monstrous imbecility; but, given a belief in the doctrine of salvation by faith, it must necessarily appear both logical and just. If the heretic *will* not believe, he is clearly wicked, for he rejects the truth and insults God. He has deliberately chosen the path to hell, and does it matter whether he travel slowly or swiftly to his destination? But does it *not* matter whether he go alone or drag down others with him to perdition? Such was the logic of the Inquisitors, and although their cruelties must be detested their consistency must be allowed.

Catholics have an infallible Church, and the Protestants an infallible Bible. Yet as the teaching of the Bible becomes a question of interpretation, the infallibility of each Church resolves itself into the infallibility of its priesthood. Each asserts that *some* belief is necessary to salvation. Religious liberty, therefore, has never entered into the imagination of either. The Protestants who revolted against the Papacy openly avowed the principle of persecution. Luther, Beza, Calvin, and Melancthon, were probably more intolerant than any Pope of their age; and if the Protestant persecutions were not, on the whole, so sanguinary as those of the Roman Catholic Church, it was simply due to the fact that Catholicism passed through a dark and ferocious period of history, while Protestantism emerged in an age of greater light and humanity. Persecution cannot always be bloody, but it always inflicts on heretics as much suffering as the sentiment of the community will tolerate.

The doctrine of salvation by faith has been more mischievous than all other delusions of theology combined. How true are the words of Pascal: "Jamais on ne fait le mal si pleinement et si gaiement que quand on le fait par un faux principe de conscience." Fortunately a nobler day is breaking. The light of truth succeeds the darkness of error. Right belief is infinitely important, but it cannot be forced. Belief is independent of will. But character is not, and therefore the philosopher approves or condemns actions instead of censuring beliefs. Theology, however, consistently clings to its old habits. "Infidels" must not be argued with but threatened, not convinced but libelled; and when these weapons are futile there ensues the persecution of silence. That serves for a time, but only for a time; it may obstruct, but it cannot prevent, the spread of unbelief. It is like a veil against the light. It may obscure the dawn to the dull-eyed and the uninquisitive, but presently the blindest sluggards in the penfolds of faith will see that the sun has risen.

LUTHER AND THE DEVIL.

"LUTHER," says Heine, "was not only the greatest, but also the most thoroughly German, hero of our history." Carlyle says that "no more valiant man, no mortal heart to be called *braver*, ever lived in that Teutonic kindred, whose character is valor." Michelet calls him "the Arminius of modern Germany." Twenty tributes to Luther's greatness might be added, all more or less memorable; but these, from three very diverse men, will suffice for our present purpose. Martin Luther *was* a great man. Whoever questions it must appeal to new definitions.

A great difference lay between the cold, saturnine Pope of Geneva and the frank, exuberant hero of the German Reformation. Their doctrines were similar; there was a likeness between their mistakes; but what a diversity in their natures! Calvin was the perfect type of the theological pedant—vain, meagre, and arid; while Luther had in him, as Heine remarks, "something aboriginal"; and the world has, after all, profited by "the God-like brutality of Brother Martin."

The nature of this great man was suited to his task. It required no great intellectual power to see through the tricks of Papal priestcraft, which had, indeed, been the jest of the educated and thoughtful for generations. But it required gigantic courage to become the spokesman of discontent, to attack an imposture which was supported by universal popular credulity, by a well-nigh omnipotent Church, and by the keen-edged, merciless swords of kings and emperors. Still more, it required an indisputable elevation of nature to attack the imposture where, as in the sale of indulgences, it threatened the very essence of personal and social morality. Hundreds of persons may be hatching a new truth in unknown concert, but when a battle for humanity has to be fought, someone must begin, and begin decisively. Luther stepped out as protagonist in the great struggle of his time; and Freethought is not so barren in great names that it need envy Brother Martin his righteous applause. Indeed, it seems to me that Freethinkers are in a position to esteem Luther more justly than Christians. Seeing what was his task, and how it demanded a stormy, impetuous nature, we can thank Luther for accomplishing it, while recognising his great defects, his faults of temper and the narrowness of his views; defects, I would add, which it were unnecessary to dwell on if Protestants did not magnify them into virtues, or if they did not illustrate the inherent vices of Christianity itself.

Strong for his life-task, Luther was weak in other respects. Like Dr. Johnson, there were strange depths in his character, but none in his intellect. He emitted many flashes of genius in writing and talking, but they all came from the heart, and chiefly from the domestic affections. He broke away from the Papacy, but he only abandoned Catholicism so far as it conflicted with the most obvious morality. He retained all its capital superstitions. Mr. Froude puts the case very mildly when he says that "Erasmus knew many things which it would have been well for Luther to have known." Erasmus would not have called Copernicus "an old fool," or have answered him by appealing to Joshua. Erasmus would not have seen a special providence in the most trifling accidents. Erasmus would not have allowed devils to worry him. Above all, Erasmus would not have pursued those who were heretics to *his* doctrine with all the animosity of a Papal bigot. Such differences induced Mr. Matthew Arnold to call Luther a Philistine of genius; just as they led Goethe to say that Luther threw back the intellectual progress of mankind for centuries. Another poet, Shelley, seems to me to have hit the precise truth in his "Ode to Liberty":

> Luther caught thy wakening glance:
> Like lightning from his leaden lance
> Reflected, it dissolved the visions of the trance
> In which, as in a tomb, the nations lay.

Shelley's epithet is perfect. Luther's lance was big and potent. It wrought terrible havoc among the enemy. But it was *leaden*. It overthrew, but it did not transfix.

This is not the place to relate how Luther played the Pope in his own way; how he persecuted the Zwinglians because they went farther than himself on the subject of the real presence; how he barked at the Swiss reformers, how he pursued Andreas Bodenstein for a difference on infant baptism; how he treated Münzer and the Anabaptists; how he hounded on the nobles to suppress the peasant revolt and " stab, kill, and strangle them without mercy "; or how he was for handing over to the executioner all who denied a single article which rested on the Scripture or the authority of the universal teaching of the Church. My purpose is to show Luther's attitude towards the Devil, witches, apparitions, and all the rest of that ghostly tribe; and in doing so I have no wish to indulge in " the most small sneer " which Carlyle reprobates; although I do think it a great pity that such a man as Luther should have been a slave to superstitions which Erasmus would have met with a wholesome jest.

Neither Jews nor witches fared any the better for the Reformation, until it had far outgrown the intention of its founders. Brother Martin hated the Jews, thought many of them sorcerers, and praised the Duke of Saxony for killing a Jew in testing a talisman. As for witches, he said, " I would have no compassion on them—I would burn them all." Poor creatures! Yet Luther was naturally compassionate. It was the fatal superstition which steeled his heart. Still there are dainty sceptics who tell us not to attack superstition. I point them to Martin Luther burning witches.

Brother Martin lived in God's presence, but they were generally three, for the Devil was seldom absent. His Satanic Majesty plagued the poor Reformer's life till he wished himself safe in heaven. Sometimes the fiend suggested impious doubts, and at other times suicide. He attributed his chronic vertigo to the Devil, because the physic he took did him no good. So familiar did the Devil become that Luther, hearing him walk overhead at night, would say " Oh, is it you?"

and go to sleep again. Once, when he was marrying an aristocratic couple, the wedding ring slipped out of his fingers at a critical moment. He was frightened, but, recovering himself, he exclaimed, "Listen, Devil, it is not your business, you are wasting your time." The famous scene in which Luther threw an inkstand at the Devil is legendary, though Coleridge, Carlyle and others have made it the theme of their eloquence; and the ink-stain still shown on the wall at Wartburg is like the stain of Rizzio's blood in Holyrood Palace.

Luther's own visions were largely due to dyspepsia and an active imagination. He said that the Devil troubled him less at night when he took a good "nightcap," which made him sleep soundly. He found that the Devil could not stand music, being a sad and sombre personage; just as, long before, music was found a sovereign recipe for the melancholia of King Saul. But the surest specific was railing and derision. When Luther called him names, or laughed at him, the Devil vanished in a huff. Brother Martin was plain-spoken at the best of times, but on these occasions he was too downright for quotation. Michelet gives a choice sample; but though the French language allows more licence than ours, he is obliged to give but the first letter of one of Luther's vigorous substantives. Brother Martin displayed a sly humor in one of his stories about Satan. A possessed person was taken into a monastery, and the devil in him said to the monks, "O my people, what have I done?"—*Popule meus, quid feci tibi?*

According to Luther, fair and foul winds were caused by good and evil spirits. He spoke of a terrible lake in Switzerland, haunted by the Devil, and said there was a similar one in his own country. If a stone was thrown into it, a frightful storm shook the whole locality. The Devil made people idiots, cripples, blind, deaf and dumb; and Luther declared that the doctors who treated such infirmities as natural had a great deal to learn in demonology. One or two of his stories of possession are extremely gruesome. With his own lusty love of life, Luther could not understand suicide, so he attributed that also to the Devil. Satan made the suicides think they were doing something else; even praying, and thus he killed them. Brother Martin, indeed, sometimes feared the Devil would twist his neck or press his skull into his brains. Nor did he shrink from the darkest developments of this superstition. He held that the Devil could assume the form of a man or a woman, cohabit with human beings of the opposite sex, and become a father or a mother. "Eight years ago," said Luther, "I saw and touched myself at Dessau a child who had no parents, and was born of the Devil. He was twelve years old, and shaped like an ordinary child. He did nothing but eat, and ate as much as three peasants or threshers. When he was touched he cried out like one possessed; if any unfortunate accident happened in the house, he rejoiced and laughed; if, on the contrary, all went well, he wept continually. I said to the princes of Anhalt, with whom I then was: If I commanded here I would have that child thrown into the Moldau, at the risk of being its murderer. But the Elector of Saxony and the princes were not of my opinion."

Here is a case in which the Doctor of Divinity, though naturally a kind man, is quite ready to take human life at the behest of a devilish superstition, while the less fanatical laymen shrink from such inhumanity. The only devil in this story is the devil of fearful ignorance and misbelief in Brother Martin. He it was who needed the exorcist, although the truth would have greatly surprised him. Carlyle may use his snarling muscles at the "apothecary's apprentice" who is able to give a scientific explanation of Luther's visions; but, after all, the unfortunate persons whom Luther would have murdered by mistake might be pardoned for preferring the apothecary's apprentice to the Protestant Pope. The fact is, the doctrine of devils, of demoniacal possession, of incubi and succubi, and of sorcery and witchcraft, was not fostered by laymen so much as by the clergy. Lecky remarks that "almost all the great works written in favor of the executions were written by ecclesiastics," and Tylor asserts that "the guilt of thus bringing down Europe intellectually and morally to the level of negro Africa" lies mainly upon the Church, Protestant being as bad as Catholic, for they vied in outraging and killing those who were doomed, by the ghastliest of superstitions, to be "for life and death of all creatures the most wretched." Eternal honor to Luther for the heroism which sent him to Worms, and made him exclaim to his dissuaders: "I will go if there are as many devils in Worms as there are tiles upon the roofs of the houses." But eternal hatred and contempt for the Creed which degraded heroes into Jack the Rippers. I say *the Creed*; for Christianity cannot be exculpated. Witchcraft, possession, and sexual intercourse between human and superhuman beings, are distinctly taught in the Bible; and if there were no other indictment of Christianity, the awful massacre and torture of millions of helpless women and children would suffice to damn it everlastingly.

BIBLE ENGLISH.

TURNING over the pages of Coleridge's "Table Talk" recently, my attention was arrested by several passages I had marked, many years ago, in that suggestive book. Two or three of these, referring to the *style* of the Bible, resuscitated some reflections I made on the first reading, and which I now venture to express: with all deference, let me add, to Coleridge's ethereal genius and magical mastery of words.

"Intense study of the Bible," he says, "will keep any writer from being *vulgar*, in point of style." Granted; and the sacred scriptures of any people and any creed would have the some influence. Vulgarity, unless it is bestial, is monkeyish. Obviously this is a characteristic alien to religion, which is based on the sense of wonder, and deals chiefly with the sublime. While the mind is absorbed by the unseen, imagination is called into play; and imagination is the antithesis of vulgarity. The unknown is also the terrible, and when the mind is alarmed there is no room for the *puerilities* of egotism. Any exaltation of feeling serves the same purpose. The most vulgar woman, in terror at a danger to her child, is lifted into the sphere of tragedy, and becomes a subject for art; nor could the lowest wretch exhibit vulgarity when committing a murder under the influence of passion. Vulgarity, in short, is self-consciousness, or at least only compatible with it; and displays itself in self-assertion at the expense of others, or in disregard or in defiance of their feelings. Now Monotheism, such as the Bible in its sublimest parts is pregnant with, naturally banishes this disposition, just in proportion as it is real. It may tolerate, and even cherish, many other evils, but not that; for vulgarity, as I understand it, is absolutely inconsistent with awe. How then do I account for the vulgarities of the Salvation Army? Simply by the fact that these people have no awe; they show the absurdities of religion without its sentiments. They are *townspeople*, used to music-halls, public-houses, street-fights, and frivolous crowds. Their antics would be impish to religionists whose awe was nurtured by hills and forests, the rising and setting sun, and the majesty of night.

Not only do we find the same austere simplicity in the Vedas, the Kurăn, and other sacred scriptures; we find it in most of the old world literature. The characteristic of modern writings is subtlety and dexterity; that of the ancient, massiveness and directness; and the same difference holds good in a comparison of the various stages of our literature. The simplicity of the Elizabethan lyrics, to say nothing of Chaucer, is only to be emulated in later ages, whose life is so much more complex, by a recluse visionary like Blake. Even when Shelley approaches it, in such songs as that of Beatrice in the last act of the "The Cenci," we feel that stream of music is crossed and shaken by subtle under-currents.

What Coleridge claims for the Bible may be claimed for all imaginative and passionate literature. Æschylus, Lucretius, Dante, Milton; how does the Bible excel these in that respect? When we come to Shakespeare we find a sublimity which transcends that of Isaiah, Ezekiel, and Job, with a pathos, a humor, and a wit, such as no Hebrew writer ever imagined. And Shakepeare's superb style triumphs easily in all these fields. Coleridge recommends the Bible as an antidote to vulgarity. I would recommend Milton as much, Dante more, and Shakespeare beyond all.

"Our version of the Bible," Coleridge elsewhere says, "has preserved a purity of meaning to many terms of natural objects. Without this holdfast, our vitiated imaginations would refine away language to mere abstractions." This is merely saying that our Bible, designed for common people centuries ago, is a monument of Saxon English. Clearly that is an accident of our translation, and not an essence of the Bible itself. As much may be said for all our ancient standards.

Coleridge admits that our New Testament is less elegant and correct than the Old, and contains "slovenly phrases which would never have come from Ben Jonson, or any other good prose writer of the day." Yet our New Testament, according to Mr. Swinburne (and there is no better judge), is translated from canine Greek into divine English. The truth is, the *style* of our Bible is owing to the translators. They lived before the hurry of our cheap periodical press, when men wrote leisurely for leisured readers. There was also no great accumulation of native literature, and scholars studied almost exclusively the masterpieces of Greece and Rome. Their sense of style was therefore superior. Read the Dedication to King James in our authorised version, then the introduction to our revised version, and see what an immense difference there is between the styles. Or read Paul's noble praise of charity in the two versions. By substituting *love* for *charity*, the revisers have vitiated the sense, and destroyed the balance of the style. Their mincing monosyllable is too weak to bear the structural weight of the clauses. A closer analysis shows that they have spoiled the passage throughout. They had no ear: in other words, no style. The old translators *had* ears, and knew other people had. Their work was meant to be read aloud, and it bears the test. That test is the supreme one, and goes deeper than hearing. Flaubert, a great master of style, always read his manuscript aloud; holding that phrases are right when they correspond to all the necessities of respiration, while ill-written phrases oppress the chest, disturb the beatings of the heart, and contravene the conditions of life. Shakespeare bears this test triumphantly. In his great passages, respiration is easy and pronunciation simple; the language is a splendid and mellifluous stream.

I venture to say in conclusion: Consult the revised version of the Bible for meaning, but read the old one for style. It is a treasury of musical and vigorous Saxon, a well of strong English undefiled; although Hebrew is a poor language, and the Greek of the New Testament is perhaps the worst ever written. But do not think, as Macaulay pretended, that the language of the Bible is sufficient for every purpose. It sustained the genius of Bunyan, but the mightier genius of Shakespeare had to draw from other sources to support its flight. Our English Bible contains six thousand words; Shakespeare's vocabulary contains nine thousand more.

LIVING BY FAITH.

What is Faith? Faith, said Paul, "is the substance of things hoped for, the evidence of things not seen." This is a faith that sensible men avoid. The man of reason may have faith, but it will be a faith according to knowledge, and not a faith that dispenses with knowledge. He believes that the sun will rise to-morrow, that the ground will remain firm under his feet, that the seasons will succeed each other in due course, and that if he tills the ground he will reap the harvest. But his belief in these things is based upon experience; his imagination extends the past into the future, and his expectations are determined by his knowledge. The future cannot indeed be demonstrated; it can only be predicted, and prediction can never amount to an absolute certitude; yet it may amount to a height of probability which is practically the same thing. Religious faith, however, is something very different. It is not belief based on evidence, but the evidence and the belief in one. The result is that persons who are full of faith always regard a demand for evidence as at once a heresy and an insult. Their faith seems to them, in the language of Paul, the very *substance* of their hopes; and they often talk of the existence of God and the divinity of Christ as being no less certain than their own existence.

Properly speaking, faith is trust. This involves a wide latitude beyond our knowledge. If we trust a friend, we have faith in him, and we act upon that sentiment. But we are sometimes deceived, and this shows that our faith was in excess of our knowledge. Sometimes, indeed, it is quite independent of knowledge. We trust people because we like them, or because they like us. This infirmity is well known to sharpers and adventurers, who invariably cultivate a pleasing manner, and generally practise the arts of flattery.

The same principle holds good in religion. It was sagaciously remarked by Hume that we ought to suspect every agreeable belief. The mass of mankind, however, are not so fastidious or discriminating. On the contrary, they frequently believe a thing because it *is* pleasant, and for no other reason. How often have we heard Christian advocates prove the immortality of the soul to the complete satisfaction of their auditors by simply harping on man's desire to live for ever! Nay, there have been many great "philosophers" who have demonstrated the same doctrine by exactly the same means.

Religious faith, to borrow a definition from *Chambers's Dictionary*, is usually "belief in the statement of another." There are a few mystics who profess to hold personal intercourse with God, but the majority of mankind take their religion on trust. They believe it because they were taught it, and those who taught them believed it for the very same reason. When you trace back the revelation to its beginning, you always find that it is derived from men who lived a long time ago, or who perhaps never lived at all. Mohammed vouches for the Koran. Yes, but who will vouch for Mohammed?

Thomas Paine well said that what is revelation to the man who receives it, is only hearsay to the man who gets it at secondhand. If anyone comes to you with a message from God, first button your pockets, and then ask him for his credentials. You will find that he has none. He can only tell you what someone else told him. If you meet the original messenger, he can only cry "thus saith the Lord," and bid you believe or be damned. To such a haughty prophet one might well reply, "My dear sir, what you say may be true, but it is very strange. Return to the being who sent you and ask him to give you better credentials. His word may be proof to you, but yours is no proof to me; and it seems reasonable to suppose that, if God had anything to tell to me, he could communicate personally to me as well as to you."

In ancient times the prophets who were thus accosted worked miracles in attestation of their mission; but our modern prophets have no such power, and therefore they can scarcely claim our belief. If they ask us why we reject what they tell us on the authority of the ancient prophets who possessed greater powers, we reply that what is a miracle to those who see it is only a story to those who hear it, and that we prefer to see the miracle ourselves. Telling us that a man rose from the dead is no reason why we should believe that three times one are one; it is only proving one wonder by another, and making a fresh draft on our credulity at every step in the demonstration.

There are men who tell us that we should live by faith. But that is impossible for all of us. The clergy live by faith, yet how could they do so if there were not others to support them? Knaves cannot exist without dupes, nor the Church without subscribers.

Living *by* faith is an easy profession. Living *on* faith, however, is more arduous and precarious. Elijah is said to have subsisted on food which was brought him by inspired ravens, but there are few of God's ministers willing to follow his example. They ask God to give them their daily bread, yet they would all shrink with horror from depending on what he sends them.

VICTOR HUGO.*

Two years and a half ago France was mourning the death of Gambetta. Every hostile voice was hushed, and the whole nation bent tearfully over the bier,

---

* May 31, 1885.

where a once mighty heart and fervent brain lay cold and still in death. Never, perhaps, since Mirabeau burned out the last of his great life had Paris been so profoundly moved. Gambetta was carried to his grave by a million of men, and in all that tremendous procession no priest figured, nor in all the funeral ceremony was there a word of God. For the first time in history a nation buried her hero without a shred of religious rites or a whisper of any other immortality than the immortality of fame.

France now mourns the death of Victor Hugo, the great poet of the Republic, as Gambetta was its great orator and statesman. These two, in their several ways, did the most to demolish the empire. Gambetta organised and led the Republican opposition, and when the *déchéance* came, he played deep for the Republic in the game of life and death, making the restoration of the empire an impossibility. But long before the young orator challenged the empire, it was arraigned before the bar of liberty and humanity by the great poet. From his lonely channel rock, in the bitter grandeur of exile, Victor Hugo hurled the lightnings and thunders of his denunciation at the political burglar of France and his parasitical minions. Practical people laughed at him, not knowing that he was more practical than they. They saw nothing but the petty present, and judged everything by its immediate success. He was nourished by sovereign principles, rooted in the depths of the human heart and blossoming in its loftiest aspirations. He was a prophet who chanted his own inspiration to the world, knowing that few would listen at first, but assured that the message would kindle some hearts, and that the living flame would leap from breast to breast till all were wrapt in its divine blaze. He scorned the base successful lie and reverenced the noble outcast truth, and he had unfaltering faith in the response which mankind would ultimately make to the voice of their rightful lord. Great he was as a poet, a romancer and a dramatist, but he was greatest as a prophet. He lived to see his message justified and his principles triumphant, and died at the ripe old age of eighty-three, amid the love and reverence of the civilised world. We are not blind to his failings; he had, as the French say, the defects of his qualities. But they do not obscure his glory. His failings were those of other men; his greatness was his own.

Victor Hugo, like Gambetta, was a Freethinker. We know he professed a belief in God, but he had no theology. His God was Nature, suffused with passion and ideality; and his conviction of "Some far-off divine event, To which the whole creation moves," was only his faith in progress, extended into the remotest future. He was a true Freethinker in his grand assertion of the majesty of reason and conscience. He appealed to the native dignity of the individual, and hated priestcraft with a perfect hatred. Lacking humor himself, and brilliant without wit, he could recognise these qualities in others, and he thought them as valid as his own weapons against the dogmas of superstition. How fine was his great word about Voltaire—"Irony incarnate for the salvation of mankind." Like Gambetta, Victor Hugo is to be buried without religious rites, according to his will. No priest is to profane the sanctity of death by mumbling idle words over his grave concerning what he is as ignorant of as the corpse at his feet. In death, as in life, the Freethinker would confront the universe alone from the impregnable rock of his manhood, convinced that

> There is no danger to a man that knows
> What life and death is : there's not any law
> Exceeds his knowledge : neither is it lawful
> That he should stoop to any other law.

Not only did Victor Hugo will that no priest should officiate at his burial, he ordered that none should approach his bed. But the carrion crows of the death-chamber were not to be deterred by his well-known wishes. The Archbishop of Paris offered to visit the

dying heretic and administer to him the supreme
unction on behalf of the Church. M. Lockroy, the
poet's son-in-law, politely declined the offer. Our
newspapers, especially the orthodox ones, regard the
Archbishop's message as a compliment. In our opinion
it was a brazen insult. Suppose Mr. Bradlaugh wrote
to say that he would gladly attend the sickbed of
Canon Wilberforce for the purpose of receiving his
confession of Atheism; would the orthodox regard it
as a compliment or an insult? We fail to see any
difference in the two cases, and we know not why
impertinence in an Atheist becomes civility in a
Christian. Fortunately, Victor Hugo's death-chamber
was not intruded upon by impudent priests. His
relatives respected his convictions the more as they
were Freethinkers themselves. No priest will consecrate his grave, but it will be hallowed by his greatness;
and what pilgrim, as he bends over the master's tomb,
will hear in the breeze, or see in the grass and flowers,
any sign that a priest's benison is wanting to his
repose?

DESECRATING A CHURCH.

THERE was a Pantheon at Rome, which was a monument of the religious tolerance of the Empire. It was
dedicated, as appears from the inscription on the
portico, by Agrippa, son-in-law to the great Augustus,
to Jupiter and all the other gods, with the same generosity that prompted the Athenians to erect an altar
to the gods that might be unknown. A niche was
afforded within its walls to every deity of the provinces

whose devotees were willing to accept the hospitality; and Christ himself might have figured with the rest, if his worshippers did not scorn all other gods but their own.

The old Pantheon still exists, and bears the name of the Rotunda. But it is no longer a Pagan temple. It was re-dedicated by Pope Boniface the Fourth, in A.D. 608, to the Virgin Mary and all the saints. Another Pope, a thousand years later, despoiled it of its ornaments, which had been spared by so many barbarian conquerors. He cast some into cannon, and with the rest formed a high altar for the Church of St. Peter.

These alterations were of course justifiable. They were all made in the interest of Christianity. What could be more proper than the transformation of Pagan temples into Christian churches? What more admirable than devoting to the worship of Christ the edifice which had echoed to the tread of the priests of Jupiter? What more pious than singing the praises of Mary and all the saints in a temple where idolaters had celebrated the glories of all the gods and goddesses of Olympus?

Such is Christian logic. But if the temples of one faith may be so transformed, why may not those of another? If Christianity had the right to devote the temples of Paganism to its own uses, why has not modern civilisation the right to devote the temples of Christianity to Secular purposes?

The Church thinks otherwise. It is at present denouncing the secularisation of the Church of St. Geneviève, in order that Victor Hugo, who died a Freethinker and was buried without religious rites, might repose in an unconsecrated place. This building is the French Pantheon. It was secularised during the Revolution, and dedicated by the Republic, not to the gods of religion, but to the heroes of liberty. When the monarchy was restored it was re-consecrated, and purged of the luciferous taint of Voltaire's dust. But now the Republic is once more established on the ruins of monarchy and imperialism, it again secularises the Church of St. Geneviève as a tomb for its mighty dead. The Church is naturally indignant, but its anathemas are powerless. God does not interpose, and the Republic is too strong. Nay, there is even a rumor that the Roman Pantheon may be secularised also, and changed into a national mausoleum, where the youth of Italy may bend reverently before the tombs of such glorious soldiers of progress as Mazzini and Garibaldi, instead of honoring the very counterfeit presentment of fabulous old saints, chiefly renowned for their laziness and dirt.

The Church of St. Geneviève is desecrated, cries the Archbishop of Paris, and special prayers are offered up to that ancient lady in heaven to avert her wrath from the infidel city which has so insulted her. In one sense the Archbishop is right. The Church is desecrated in the strict etymological meaning of the word. It has been converted from sacred to secular uses. But in the secondary meaning of the word the building is not desecrated, but honored, by being made a fit receptacle for the mortal remains of Victor Hugo.

A government decree and the removal of the cross on top of the church were the only steps necessary to its desecration. The consecrated character of the temple is gone. To the carnal eye the structure remains unchanged, within and without, except for the loss of a crucifix; but it is quite possible that a priestly nose would be able to scent the absence of the Spirit. The Holy Ghost has fled, angels no more haunt the nave and aisles, and St. Geneviève hides her poor head in grief and humiliation. No doubt; yet we dare say the building will stand none the less firmly, and if it should ever be pulled down, its materials would fetch as much in the market as if they were saturated with divinity.

Consecration is, after all, nothing but a priestly trick. What sensible man believes that the Holy

Ghost, if such a being exist, is at the beck and call of every Catholic or Protestant bishop? Can the " universal spirit " dwell exclusively in certain places? Can the third person of the Trinity have sunk into such an abject state as to dodge in and out of buildings, according as he is wanted or not? Is there any difference that the nose, or any other sensitive organ, can detect between a consecrated church and an unconsecrated chapel? Can the geologist or the chemist discern any difference between the consecrated and the unconsecrated division in a cemetery? Is the earth affected by priestly mutterings? Do the corpses lie any more peacefully, or decompose any more slowly, for the words pronounced over the mould that covers them? Or is there any appreciable virtue in the consecrated water, with which the Protestant and Catholic are alike baptised, and with which the latter sprinkles himself periodically as a preservative against evil? Reason finds no difference; it is perceived only by Faith, which may be defined as the faculty which enables a man to see what does not exist.

WALT WHITMAN.*

WALT WHITMAN's death can have taken no one by surprise. For years he had been at the brink of the grave, and the end comes as a relief. A great soul may be cheerful, or at least serene, in all circumstances; but there is neither pleasure nor dignity in living on as the ghost of one's self.

* April, 1892.

Few superber specimens of physical manhood than Walt Whitman's have appeared on this planet. "He looks like a man," said Abraham Lincoln, as his gaze followed the poet past a window of the White House. Whitman stood six feet two, his limbs and torso were splendid, and his head was magnificently proportioned. His vitality must have been wonderful, and his health was absolutely perfect until after the War, during which he too assiduously nursed the sick and wounded, to the lasting detriment of his phenomenal constitution. The flame of his life burnt on for another thirty years, but his strength was seriously undermined, and he is far better entitled to be called a martyr than many who have more cheaply earned the distinction.

Walt Whitman's great personality can hardly be disputed. He impressed himself as something colossal on all who came into close contact with him. The magnetism of his presence in the military hospitals was more sanative than the doctors' physic. Men, women, and children felt glad and satisfied in his company. His large, frank, healthy nature radiated a perpetual benediction. One who knew him intimately has said that he never saw upon Whitman's features any trace of mean or evil passions. The man was thoroughly wholesome. Even his occasionally free utterances on sexuality are only sins against decorum. They do not violate nature. He never spoke on this subject with the slobbery grin of the voluptuary, or the leer of prurience. He was at such moments simply unreticent. Meaning no harm, he suspected none. In this respect he belonged to a less self-conscious antiquity, when nothing pertaining to man was common or unclean, and even the worship of the powers of generation was not without dignity and solemnity.

Some of the foremost Englishmen of our time have acknowledged Whitman's greatness and sanity—notably Carlyle, Ruskin, and Tennyson. Mr. Swinburne is the only one who has unsaid his praise.

Tennyson's intimacy with Whitman—always through correspondence—was simply beautiful. A superficial reader of human nature might have inquired what they had in common—the rough, amorphous American poet, and the exquisite English poet, a flower of millenniums of culture. But there is something deeper than form. It is substance. There is something deeper than language. It is manhood. And on the common ground of the deeper things of life, the American and English poets—otherwise so diverse—clasped hands, as it were, across the sundering ocean.

Whitman's claim to be considered a great poet, or even a poet at all, has been the subject of hot dispute. But such questions are not so settled. Only give time enough, and every writer falls by mere gravitation into his proper place, from which all the controversies in the world can never shift him. Where the evidence is largely subjective, as it must be in appraising genius, there is sure to be much in our judgment that is incommunicable. The logic of events, as we say in politics; or the proof of the pudding, as we say in the vernacular; is not so brilliant as logical sword-play, but it has the merit of being decisive.

Whitman's poetry looks strange to a reader accustomed to conventional models. It positively offends his eyesight. The ear may detect a certain rhythm, but where are the set lengths of orthodox versification? Here, however, there lurks a fallacy. Poetry is not the antithesis of prose. The antithesis of prose is verse. Some of the finest and noblest poetry in the world's literature is not cast in rhyme, though rhythm —often subtler than all possible rules—is indispensable. Yet there is something precious in poetical form; ay, and something durable. Many an exquisite lyric, with no great depth of feeling or reach of thought, has come down the stream of time, and will float upon it for ever. No doubt Dr. Johnson was right in calling it a waste of time to carve cherry-stones, but precious stones are the more valued and admired for the art of the lapidary. Whitman did not cultivate versification. He almost despised it. He sneered at " dulcet rhymes." Yet this may hinder his access to posterity. Mr. Meredith hints as much in his sonnet entitled " An Orson of the Muse," which surely refers to Whitman. He allows him to be the Muse's son, though he will not wear her livery.

> Him, whom he blows of Earth, and Man, and Fate,
> The Muse will hearken to with graver ear
> Than many of her train can waken : him
> Would fain have taught what fruitful things and dear
> Must sink beneath the tidewaves, of their weight,
> If in no vessel built for sea they swim.

That Whitman, however, could do great things with rhythm, and without rhyme, is proved by his " Funeral Hymn of President Lincoln," which James Thomson ranked with Shelley's " Adonais," and Mr. Swinburne called " the most sublime nocturne ever chanted in the cathedral of the world." That this is a great poem, and will live, we have not the slightest doubt. Some other of Whitman's poems will doubtless live with it, but whole masses of his poetry will probably sink to the bottom—not, however, before doing their work and delivering their message.

Because of his want of form, Whitman suffers more than other poets in extracts. We shall make none, but refer the reader to the whole body of his poetry. Some of it is almost wearisome ; the rest will repay study. It contains the utterance of a great soul, full of love and friendship, patriotism and humanity, brooding over the everlasting problems of life and death. Untrammelled by schools and systems, Whitman was a true Freethinker. Cosmopolitan as he was, he preached the gospel of individuality.

> "This is what you shall do : love the earth and the sun and the animals, despise riches, give alms to everyone that asks, stand up for the stupid and the crazy, devote your income and labor to others, hate tyrants, argue not concerning God, have patience and indulgence towards the people, take off your hat to nothing known or unknown, or to any man or number of

men, go freely with powerful uneducated persons and with the young and mothers of families, re-examine all you have been told at school or church or in any book, dismiss whatever insults your own soul; and your very flesh shall be a great poem, and have the richest fluency, not only in its words, but in the silent lines of its lips and face, and between the lashes of your eyes, and in every motion and joint of your body."

Whitman appealed to the brotherhood of all and the dignity of each. He declared he would have nothing which every other man might not have on equal terms. The business of the great poet was "to cheer up slaves and horrify despots." Men, too, should keep in close communion with Nature, yet always feel that they could "be good or grand only of the consciousness of the supremacy within them."

"What do you think is the grandeur of storms and dismemberments, and the deadliest battles and wrecks, and the wildest fury of the elements, and the power of the sea, and the motion of nature, and of the throes of human desires, and dignity and hate and love? It is that something in the soul which says—Rage on, whirl on, I tread master here and everywhere; master of the spasms of the sky and of the shatter of the sea, of all terror and all pain."

America, perhaps even more than England, has need of Whitman's teaching as the poet of Democracy. He derided "the mania of owning things," he scorned distinctions of caste and class, he sang the divineness of comradeship—and, what is more, he practised it. Full-blooded, strong-limbed, rich-brained, large-hearted men and women are a nation's best products, and if a nation does not yield them, its wealth will only hasten its doom and pollute its grave.

TENNYSON AND THE BIBLE.*

WE owe no apology for speaking of the dead poet as "Tennyson." This is how he will be known by posterity. The rank is but the guinea's stamp, and in this case it was not requisite. A true poet's gold can neither be made more precious nor more current by empty titles. In our opinion, it is a degradation, instead of an honor, for one of nature's aristocrats to herd with the artificial nobility of an hereditary peerage. We also take the opportunity of regretting that Tennyson ever became Poet Laureate. The court poet should not survive the court dwarf and the court jester. It is painful to see a great writer grinding out professional odes, and bestowing the excrements of his genius on royal nonentities. The preposterous office of Poet Laureate should now be abolished. No poet should write for a clique or a coterie; he should appeal directly to the heart of the nation.

Tennyson's funeral took place at Westminster Abbey. The heads of that establishment, following the example set by Dean Stanley, now act as bodysnatchers. They appropriate the corpses of distinguished men, whether they believed or disbelieved the doctrines of the service read over their coffins. Charles Darwin's body is buried there—the great Agnostic, who repudiated Christianity; Robert Browning's too—the poet who said "I am no Christian" to Robert Buchanan. Carlyle took care that his corpse should not join the museum. Tennyson's, however, is now in the catalogue; and, it must be admitted, with more plausibility than in the case of Browning—with far more than in the case of Darwin.

---

* October, 1892.

Christian pulpiteers, all over the country, have been shouting their praises of Tennyson as a Christian poet. They are justified in making the most of a man of genius when they possess one. We do not quarrel with them. We only beg to remark that they have overdone it. The Christianity of Tennyson is a very different thing from the Christianity they vend to the credulous multitude.

There is no real evidence that Tennyson accepted the legendary part of Christianity. Even in "In Memoriam," which was published forty-three years ago, the thought is often extremely Pantheistic. It is nearly always so in the later poems. God, not Christ, became more and more the object of the poet's adoration. "Strong Son of God, immortal Love"—the first line of the earlier poem—does not necessarily mean Christ; while the exclamation, "Ring in the Christ that is to be," is more symbolic than personal. There is also a strong hope, rather than the certitude, of a future life. No thoroughly convinced Christian could have written of

> The Shadow cloaked from head to foot,
> Who keeps the keys of all the creeds.

Nay, the very deity of Christ is held loosely, if at all, in the thirty-third section, where he

> Whose faith has centre everywhere,
> Nor cares to fix itself to form,

is bidden to leave his sister undisturbed when she prays; the poet exclaiming

> Oh, sacred be the flesh and blood
> To which she links a truth divine!

In the last line of the next stanza this "sacred flesh and blood" of Christ (it is to be presumed) is called "a type"—which is a wide departure from orthodox Christianity. And what shall we say of the final lines of the whole poem?

> One God, one law, one element,
> And one far-off divine event,
> To which the whole creation moves.

Like other passages of "In Memoriam," it is a distinct anticipation of the thought of "The Higher Pantheism," "Flower in the Crannied Wall," "De Profundis," and "The Ancient Sage."

Much has been made of the "Pilot" in one of Tennyson's last poems, "Crossing the Bar."

> I hope to see my Pilot face to face
> When I have crossed the bar.

This has been treated as a reference to Christ; but a friend of Tennyson's, writing in the *Athenæum*, says that the reference was really to the poet's son, Lionel Tennyson, who "crossed the bar" of death some years previously. How much more natural and human is the reference in the light of this explanation! Yet it appears, after all, from a later letter to the press by Tennyson's surviving son, that he *did* mean Christ. This is not, however, a confession of orthodoxy. The sentiment might be shared by men like the venerable Dr. Martineau, who deny the deity of Christ and strongly dissent from many time-honored Christian teachings.

Tennyson most assuredly revolted against the brutalities of Christianity; which, by the way, are countenanced by very explicit texts in the New Testament. He did not approve the text, "Great is your reward in heaven." He was above such huckstering. He sang of Virtue—

> She desires no isles of the blest, no quiet seats of the just,
> To rest in a golden grove, or to bask in a summer sky.
> Give her the wages of going on, and not to die.

A noble petition! though in the teeth of a too patent destiny.

The doctrine of eternal Hell he first turned from, then denounced, and finally despised. It was for wavering as to this hideous dogma that the Rev. F. D. Maurice got into trouble with his College. He was godfather to Tennyson's little boy, and the poet invited him, in exquisitely charming verse, to share his hospitality.

> For, being of that honest few,
> Who give the Fiend himself his due,
>   Should eighty-thousand college-councils
> Thunder "Anathema," friend, at you;
>
> Should all our churchmen foam in spite
> At you, so careful of the right,
>   Yet one lay-hearth would give you welcome
> (Take it and come) to the Isle of Wight.

—Tennyson had already, in "In Memoriam," proclaimed himself a Universalist, as Browning did afterwards in his powerful lines on the old Morgue at Paris. He had expressed the hope

> That nothing walks with aimless feet;
>   That not one life should be destroyed,
>   Or cast as rubbish to the void,
> When God hath made the pile complete;
>
> That not a worm is cloven in vain;
>   That not a moth with vain desire
>   Is shrivelled in a fruitless fire,
> Or but subserves another's gain.

Such a poet could never see the divinity of the wicked, awful words, "Depart from me, ye cursed, into everlasting fire." He denounced it in "Despair," a poem of his old age. Well does he make the Agnostic cry out to the minister—

> What! I should call on that Infinite Love that has served us so well?
> Infinite cruelty rather that made everlasting Hell,
> Made us, foreknew us, foredoom'd us, and does what he will with his own;
> Better our dead brute mother who never has heard us groan!

This is fierce denunciation, but it pales before the attack on Hell in "Rizpah"; that splendid poem, which is perhaps the very noblest effort of Tennyson's genius; outweighing hundreds of Balaclava charges and sea-fights; outshining the flawless perfection of "Maud":—a poem written in heart's blood and immortal tears, with a wondrously potent and subtle imagination, and a fire of humanity to burn up whole mountains of brutal superstitions.

L

The passionate words of the poor old dying mother, full of a deathless love for her boy who was hung, go straight as an arrow to its mark, through all the conventions of society and all the teachings of the Church.

Election, Election and Reprobation—it's all very well,
But I go to-night to my boy, and I shall not find him in Hell.
. . . . . .
And if *he* be lost—but to save *my* soul, that is all your desire;
Do you think that I care for *my* soul if my boy be gone to the fire?

Tennyson gives the very essence of the moral revolt against Hell. Human nature has so developed in sympathy that the sufferings of others, though out of sight, afflict our imaginations. We loathe the spectacle of Abraham and Lazarus gazing complacently on the torture of Dives. Once it was not so. Those who were " saved " had little or no care for the " damned." But the best men and women of to-day do not want to be saved alone. They want a common salvation or none. And the mother's heart, which the creeds have trampled upon, hates the thought of any happiness in Heaven while son or daughter is agonising in Hell.

It is perfectly clear that Tennyson was far from an orthodox Christian. Quite as certainly he was not a Bibliolator. He read the Bible, of course; and so did Shelley. There are fine things in it, amidst its falsehoods and barbarities; and the English version is a monument of our literature. We regard as apocryphal, however, the story of Tennyson's telling a boy, " Read the Bible and Shakespeare; the one will teach you how to speak to God, and the other how to speak to your fellow-men." Anyhow, when the poet came to die, he did not ask for the Bible and he did ask for Shakespeare. The copy he habitually used was handed to him; he opened it at " Cymbeline," one of the most pagan of Shakespeare's plays; he read a little, and then held the book until Death came with the fall of " tired eyelids upon tired eyes."

It was a poetic death, and a pagan death. There

lay the aged, world-weary poet; artificial light was withdrawn, and the moonlight streamed through the window upon his noble figure. Wife and son, doctors and nurses, were silent around him. And as Death put the last cold touch on the once passionate heart, it found him still clasping the book of the mighty magician.* Let it be also noted that no Christian priest was at his bedside. He needed not the mumblings of a smaller soul to aid him in his last extremity. Hope he may have had, but no fear. His life ended like a long summer day, slowly dying into night.

CHRIST'S OLD COAT.

THE little town of Trier (Trèves) will soon wear a festive appearance. Pilgrims will be flocking to it from all parts of Germany, and God knows from where besides. Its handful of inhabitants have obtained licenses to open hotels and restaurants; every inch of available space has been let, so that whirligigs, panoramas, and menageries have to be refused the sites

---

* The present Lord Tennyson wrote as follows to Sir Arthur Hodgson, Chairman of the Shakespeare's Birthplace Trustees : "I beg to convey from my mother and myself our grateful acknowledgment to the Executive Committee of Shakespeare's Birthplace for their most kind expression of sympathy and for their beautiful wreath. My father was reading 'King Lear,' 'Troilus and Cressida,' and 'Cymbeline' through the last days of his life. On Wednesday he asked for Shakespeare. I gave him the book, but said, 'You must not try to read.' He answered, 'I have opened the book.' I looked at the book at midnight when I was sitting by him, lying dead on the Thursday, and found he had opened on one of the passages which he had called the tenderest in Shakespeare. We could not part with this volume, but buried a Shakespeare with him. We had the book enclosed in a metal box and laid by his side.—Yours faithfully, HALLAM TENNYSON"

they apply for; every room in the town is to be let, more or less furnished; and not only is the tram company doubling its line, but the railway company is constructing special stations for special trains.

All this excitement springs from a superstitious source. After an interval of several years the Church will once more exhibit an old rag, which it calls the Holy Coat, and which it pretends is the very garment we read of in the Gospels. Such a precious relic is, of course, endowed with supernatural qualities. It will heal the sick, cure cripples, and, let us hope, put brains into idiotic heads. Hence the contemplated rush to Trier, where more people will congregate to see Christ's coat than ever assembled to hear him preach or see him crucified.

The pilgrims will not be allowed to examine the Holy Coat. Few of them, perhaps, would be inclined to do so. They have the faith which removes mountains, and swallowing a coat is but a trifle. Nor would the Church allow a close inspection of this curious relic, any more than it would allow a chemist to examine the bottle in which the blood of St. Januarius annually liquefies. The Holy Coat will be held up by priests at a discreet and convenient distance; the multitude of fools will fall before it in ecstatic adoration; and the result will be the usual one in such cases, a lightening of the devotees' pockets to the profit of Holy Mother Church.

According to the Gospels, the Prophet of Nazareth had a seamless overcoat. Perhaps it was presented to him by one of the rich women who ministered unto him of their substance. Perhaps it was a birthday gift from Joseph of Arimathæa. Anyhow he had it, unless the Gospels lie; and, with the rest of his clothes, it became the property of his executioners. Those gentlemen raffled for it. Which of them won it we are not informed. Nor are we told what he did with it. It would be a useless garment to a Roman soldier, and perhaps the warrior who won the raffle sold it to a second-hand clothes-dealer. This, however, is merely a conjecture. Nothing is known with certainty. The seamless overcoat disappeared from view as decisively as the person who wore it.

For many hundreds of years it was supposed to have gone the way of other coats. No one thought it would ever be preserved in a Church museum. But somehow it turned up again, and the Church got possession of it, though the Church could not tell how and when it was found, or where it had been while it was lost. One coat disappeared; hundreds of years afterwards another coat was found; and it suited the Church to declare them the same.

At that time the Church was "discovering" relics with extraordinary success and rapidity. Almost everything Christ ever used (or didn't use) came to light. His baby linen, samples of his hair and teeth, and the milk he drew from Mary's breast, the shoes he wore into Jerusalem, fragments of the twelve baskets' full of food after the miracle of the loaves and fishes, the dish from which he ate the last supper, the thorns that crowned his brow, the sponge put to his lips on the cross, pieces of the cross itself—these and a host of other relics were treasured at various churches in Europe, and exhibited with unblushing effrontery. Even the prepuce of Jesus, amputated at his circumcision, was kept at Rome.

Several churches boasted the same articles. John the Baptist's body was in dozens of different places, and the finger with which he pointed to Jesus as his successor was shown, in a fine state of preservation, at Besancon, Toulouse, Lyons, Bourges, Macon, and many other towns.

John Calvin pointed out, in his grim *Treatise on Relics*, that the Holy Coat of Christ was kept in several churches. In our own time, a book on this subject has been written by H. von Sybel, who proves that the Trier coat is only one of twenty that were exhibited. All were authentic, and all were guaranteed by the same authority. Holy Mother Church lied and cheated without a twinge of compunction.

Nineteen Holy Coats have gone. The twentieth is the last of the tribe. While it *pays* it will be exhibited. When it ceases to pay, the Church will quietly drop it. By and bye the Church will swear it never kept such an article in stock.

Superstition dies hard, and it always dies viciously. The ruling passion is strong in death. A journalist has just been sent to prison for casting a doubt on the authenticity of this Holy Coat. Give the Catholic Church its old power again, and all who laughed at its wretched humbug would be choked with blood.

Protestants, as well as Freethinkers, laugh at Catholic relics. Were we to quote from some of the old English " Reformers," who carried on a vigorous polemic against Catholic " idolatry," we should be reproached for soiling our pages unnecessarily. John Calvin himself, the Genevan pope, declared that so many samples of the Virgin Mary's milk were exhibited in Europe that " one might suppose she was a wet nurse or a cow."

Freethinkers, however, laugh at the miracles of Protestantism, as well as those of the Catholic Church. They are all of a piece, in the ultimate analysis. It is just as credible that Christ's Coat would work miracles, as that Elisha's bones restored a corpse to life, or that Paul's handkerchiefs cured the sick and diseased. All such things belong to the same realm of pious imagination. Thus, while the Protestant laughs at the Catholic, the Freethinker laughs at both.

CHRIST'S COAT, NUMBER TWO.

JESUS CHRIST is urgently required on earth again, to settle the pious dispute between Trèves and Argenteuil as to which possesses the real seamless coat that was taken from him at the Crucifixion and raffled for by the Roman soldiers. No one but the second person of the Trinity, unless it be the first or third person of that three-headed monstrosity, is adequate to the settlement of this distracting quarrel. Even the Papacy, which represents the Holy Trinity on earth, is at variance with itself. Pope Leo favors Trèves, and the wicked pilgrims who visit that little old town are to obtain absolution, if they do not forget to "pray for the extirpation of erroneous doctrines." Pope Pius, his predecessor, however, favored Argenteuil. A portion of the Holy Coat treasured in the church there was sent to him, and in return for the precious gift he forwarded a well-blessed and marvellously-decorated wax taper, which is still on show in a fine state of preservation.

When Popes differ, ordinary people, like pious Christians, and even the editors of Freethought journals, may be excused if they hesitate to commit themselves. One of these coats *may* be the true one, though the evidence is all against it, being in fact of such a shaky nature that it would hardly suffice to substantiate a claim to a bunch of radishes. But *both* of them *cannot* be authentic, and the problem is, which is the very coat that Jesus wore? Now it is obvious that no one—barring his two colleagues aforesaid—can possibly determine this question but himself. His re-appearance on earth is therefore most desirable; nay, it is absolutely necessary, unless a lot of people who would fain bow before the cast-off clothes of their Redeemer are either to stay at home in a state of dubiety or to incur the risk of kneeling before a mouldy old rag that perchance belonged to a Moorish slave or a Syrian water-carrier—in any case, to a dog of an infidel who spat at the very name of Christ, for such raiment was never worn by the worshippers of the Nazarene.

If Christ is coming to decide this great and grave problem, he will have to make haste, for Argenteuil is already on the war-path. Its Holy Coat is being exhibited before that of Trèves, and thousands of pilgrims are giving Number Two the preference. Presently the Trèves relic will attract its thousands, and the spectacle will be positively scandalous. Two Richmonds in the field were nothing to two Christ's Coats, each pretending to be the real article, and each blessed by a Pope. For the sake of decency as well as truth, Christ should peremptorily interfere. It is difficult to see how he can refrain. The Second Advent may therefore be expected before the date assigned by Prophet Baxter, and we shall probably soon hear the faithful singing "Lo he comes in clouds descending."

Why should he not come? we may ask the Catholics. His mother has often appeared, if we may believe the solemn affidavits of priests and bishops, backed up by the Holy See. Why should he not come? we may also ask the Protestants. His second coming is an article of their faith; it is plainly taught in the New Testament, and was recently propounded by Mr. Spurgeon as part of the irreducible minimum of the Christian faith. That he will come, then, may be taken for granted; and what better opportunity could be desired than the present? Surely the faithful, all over Europe—ay, and in America, to say nothing of Asia, Africa, and Australia—will cry like one man, " Come Lord Jesus, quickly come! Tell us, oh tell us, which of these mouldy old rags did once grace thy holy shoulders? Save us, oh save us, from the pain, the ignominy of adoring a dirty relic of some unknown sinner, who perhaps blasphemed thy holy name. Lighten our darkness, we beseech thee, O Lord !"

Meanwhile we may point out that, if Christ does not come and adjudicate between Trèves and Argenteuil, a multitude of Christians will certainly go on a fool's errand. Our private opinion is that all will do so who visit either of these places. Nevertheless they will no doubt congratulate themselves, if they go to Trèves, on winning absolution. The Holy Father at Rome, who has a supernatural dispensing power, promises to wipe out the record of their sins. Liars, cheats, seducers, adulterers, and undetected assassins, may take a trip, perform genuflexions before something in a glass case, and return home with a clean record. Who can conceive an easier method of avoiding the consequences of wickedness? As for the prayer which the pilgrims are to offer up for "the extirpation of erroneous doctrines," it will cost them very little effort, for sinners who are washed clean with such delightful celerity are not likely to be in love with "erroneous doctrines" that declare the Pope's dispensing power a sham, and sternly tell men that the consequences of action, whether good or bad, are inevitable. We very much doubt, however, if "erroneous doctrines" will disappear through the prayers of the pilgrims or the curses of the Pope. Scepticism will probably gain by the spectacle of two rival Coats of Christ, both exhibited at the same time, both attracting crowds of devotees, and both enjoying the Papal blessing. It will bring superstition into still further contempt, and promote the rejection of a creed which has ever traded on ignorance and credulity.

SCOTCHED, NOT SLAIN.

THOSE who have read the foregoing articles on the Holy Coat exhibitions at Trèves and Argenteuil may think that enough space has been devoted to such a ridiculous subject. It is possible, however, that the present article will induce them to alter that opinion.

Hitherto we have treated this outburst of Christian superstition with jocosity, but there is a serious aspect of it which must not be neglected. Christianity has often made Freethinkers laugh, but not unfrequently it has made them weep tears of blood. Absurdity is not always a laughing matter. There was a comic side to the orthodox persecution of Charles Bradlaugh— but it killed him. Bigotry and superstition are fit subjects for jest and ridicule; when they gain power, however, they are apt to substitute agony for laughter. Celsus ridiculed Christianity in the second century; in the fourth his writings were absolutely destroyed, and those who shared his opinions, and dared to express them, were on the high road to the prison and the stake.

More recent events teach the same lesson. Thomas Paine treated Christianity not only with trenchant argument, but also with brilliant derision. For this he suffered ostracism and calumny, and for publishing the *Age of Reason* Richard Carlile, his wife, his sister, and his shopmen rotted in English gaols. The *Freethinker* derided Christian absurdities, and its conductors were sent to herd with criminals in a Christian prison. Nearly everyone thought, as Sir James Stephen declared in a legal text-book, that the Blasphemy Laws were obsolete; but it was proved by the inexorable logic of fact that laws are never obsolete until they are repealed. While the Blasphemy Laws exist they are always liable to enforcement. They are the standing menace of an absurd creed to those who smile at it too ostentatiously.

Let us extend the same line of reflection to this Holy Coat business. Contemptible as it is to the eye of reason, it excites the piety of millions of persons who never reasoned on religion in the whole course of their lives. Hundreds of thousands of men and women will visit these sham relics of a Savior whose own existence is open to dispute. Superstition will be stirred to its depths. The bestial instinct of spiritual slavery inherited from ancient semi-human progenitors will be intensely stimulated. The sacred function of priests will be heightened and intensified. Nor must it be forgotten that the pecuniary offerings of the pilgrims will fill the coffers of Holy Mother Church, who promises heaven to her dupes and seizes wealth and power for herself on earth.

Superstition is scotched, but not slain. It has life enough to be a peril to civilisation. The faith which wrecked " the grandeur that was Greece and the glory that was Rome "—the faith which buried the science, art, philoscphy and literature of antiquity under a monstrous heap of brutal rubbish, out of which they were slowly and painfully excavated after the lapse of a thousand years—this same faith is still a danger to the highest welfare of mankind; to its reason, its conscience, its sense of dignity, and its spirit of brotherhood; above all, to freedom of thought, which is the sole guarantee of real and durable progress.

If we turn to Russia, we see at a single glance the fruits of superstition and its twin-sister tyranny. The Czar is the head of the Church and the head of the State; not like Queen Victoria, whose sacred function is only indicated in Latin on our coinage, but in literal, prosaic fact. By means of a swarm of ignorant, and often drunken and immoral priests, the masses of the people are kept in wretched subjection—hewers of wood and drawers of water, toilers for the huge army of officials, aristocrats, and princes—and conscripts for

the army; while the best and noblest, in whom there
still throbs the pulse of freedom, blacken the highways
to the mines of Siberia, where hell is more than realised
on earth, and the dreams of sour-blooded theologians
are outdone in misery and horror.

Over the rest of Europe, even in France, the secular
State is often as insecure as the footsteps of travellers
over thin crusts of volcanic soil. Bismarck, the Titan,
whose great work, with all its defects and failings, may
appeal from the clamorous passing hour to the quiet
verdict of history, only kept the Catholic Church and
its Jesuits in check for a generation. He could not
impair its vitality nor diminish its latent power. It is
in Germany that the Coat of Christ is being exhibited,
with priests and professors joining hands at the brazen
ceremony of imposture: in Germany that myriads of
pilgrims are wending their way to the shrine of an
idolatry as ignominious as anything that Christianity
ever supplanted.

Even in France the one great danger to the Republic
is Christian superstition. It is the Church, her priests
and her devotees, that furnish the real strength of
every reactionary movement. That consummate char-
latan, General Boulanger, took to going to church and
cultivating orthodoxy when at the height of his aspiration for power. Happily he was defeated by the men
of light and leading. Happily, too, the ablest and most
trusted leaders of public life in France are on the side
of Freethought. It is this, more than anything else,
that makes the country of Voltaire the beacon of
civilisation as well as the " martyr of democracy."

Charles Bradlaugh, on a very solemn occasion,
warned the Freethought party that even in England
their great fight would ultimately be with the Catholic
Church. He knew that superstition was scotched, but
he also knew it was far from slain. While Freethinkers are laughing at this exhibition of old rags,
called the Coat of Christ, they should pause for a
moment to consider the serious meaning of such a

grotesque display of superstition in the land of Goethe and Heine, and in the age of Darwin. Let us jest round our camp-fires, but let us grip our sword-hilts as we hear the cries, the jingle of weapons, and the tramp of men in the camp of our enemy.

GOD-MAKING.

"MAN is certainly stark mad; he cannot make a flea, and yet he will be making gods by dozens." So wrote honest Montaigne, the first great sceptic in modern history, who was so far in advance of his age that he surprised the world by venturing to doubt whether it was after all a just and sensible thing to burn a man alive for differing from his neighbors.

The history of that mental aberration which is called religion, and a survey of the present state of the world, from the fetish worshipper of central Africa to the super-subtle Theist of educated Europe, furnish us with countless illustrations of the truth of Montaigne's exclamation. God-making has always been a prevalent pastime, although it has less attraction for the modern than for the ancient mind. It was a recreation in which everyone could indulge, whether learned or illiterate, young or old, rich or poor. All the material needed to fashion gods of was ignorance, and there was always an unlimited stock of that article. The artificer was imagination, a glorious faculty, which is the highest dower of the creative artist and the scientific discoverer, and in their service is fruitful in usefulness and beauty, but which in the service of theology is a frightful curse, filling the mental world with fantastic monsters who waylay and devour.

Common people, however, who did the work of the world, were not able to do much god-making. Their leisure and ability were both limited. But they had a large capacity for admiring the productions of others, and their deficiencies were supplied by a special class of men, called priests, who were set apart for the manufacture of deities, and who devoted their time and their powers to the holy trade. This pious division of labor, this specialisation of function, still continues. Carpenters and tailors, grocers and butchers, who are immersed all the week in labor or business, have no opportunity for long excursions in the field of divinity; and therefore they take their religion at second hand from the priest on Sunday. It was not the multitude, but the sacred specialists, who built up the gigantic and elaborate edifice of theology, which is a purely arbitrary construction, deriving all its design and coherence from the instinctive logic of the human mind, that operates alike in a fairy tale and in a syllogism.

Primitive man used conveniently-shaped flints before he fashioned flint instruments; discovery always preceding invention. In like manner he found gods before he made them. A charm resides in some natural object, such as a fish's tooth, a queer-shaped pebble, or a jewel, and it is worn as an amulet to favor and protect. This is fetishism. By-and-bye counterfeits are made of animals and men, or amalgams of both, and the fetishistic sentiment is transferred to these. This is the beginning of polytheism. And how far it extends even into civilised periods, let the superstitions of Europe attest. The nun who tells her beads, and the lady who wears an ornamental crucifix, are to some extent fetishists; while the Catholic worship of saints is only polytheism in disguise.

Reading the Bible with clear eyes, we see that the ancient Jews worshipped gods of their own making, which were handed down as family relics. When

Jacob made tracks after sucking his uncle dry, Rachel carried off the poor old fellow's teraphim, and left him without even a god to worship. Jahveh himself, who has since developed into God the Father, was originally nothing but an image in an ark. Micah, in the book of Judges, makes himself a houseful of gods, and hires a Levite as his domestic chaplain. How long the practice persisted we may judge from the royal scorn which Isaiah pours on the image-mongers, who hewed down cedars and cypresses, oaks and ashes, some for fuel and some for idols. Let us hear the great prophet: "He burneth part thereof in the fire; with part thereof he eateth flesh; he roasteth roast, and is satisfied: yea, he warmeth himself, and saith, Aha, I am warm, I have seen the fire: And the residue thereof he maketh a god, even his graven image: he falleth down unto it, and worshippeth it, and prayeth unto it, and saith, Deliver me, for thou art my god."

Twenty-six centuries have elapsed since Isaiah wrote that biting satire, yet image-worship still prevails over three-fourths of the world; and even in Christian countries, to use Browning's phrase, we "see God made and eaten every day." A wave of the hand and a muttered spell, change bread or wafer and port-wine into the body and blood of Christ, which are joyously consumed by hi cannibal worshippers.

Not even the higher divinities of the greater faiths are exempt from the universal law. They are not creatures of man's hand, yet they are creatures of his brain. What are they but his own fancies, brooded on till they become facts of memory, and seem to possess an objective existence? The process is natural and easy. A figment of the imagination may become intensely real. Have we not a clearer idea of Hamlet and Othello than of half our closest acquaintances? Feuerbach went straight to the mark when he aimed to prove "that the powers before which man crouches are the creatures of his own limited, ignorant, uncultured and timorous mind, and that in especial the being whom man sets over against himself as a separate supernatural existence in his own being."

Yes, all theology is anthropomorphism—the making of gods in man's image. What is the God of our own theology, as Matthew Arnold puts it, but a magnified man? We cannot transcend our own natures, even in imagination; we can only interpret the universe in the terms of our own consciousness, nor can we endow our gods with any other attributes than we possess ourselves. When we seek to penetrate the "mystery of the infinite," we see nothing but our own shadow and hear nothing but the echo of our own voice.

As we are so are our gods, and what man worships is what he himself would be. The placid Egyptian nature smiles on the face of the sphinx. The gods of India reflect the terror of its heat and its beasts and serpents, the fertility of its soil, and the exuberance of its people's imagination. The glorious Pantheon of Greece—

> Praxitelean shapes, whose marble smiles
> Fill the hushed air with everlasting love—

embodies the wise and graceful fancies of the noblest race that ever adorned the earth, compared with whose mythology the Christian system is a hideous nightmare. The Roman gods wear a sterner look, befitting their practical and imperial worshippers, and Jove himself is the ideal genius of the eternal city. The deities of the old Scandinavians, whose blood tinges our English veins, were fierce and warlike as themselves, with strong hands, supple wrists, mighty thews, lofty stature, grey-blue eyes and tawny hair. Thus has it ever been. So Man created god in his own image, in the image of Man created he him; male and female created he them.

GOD AND THE WEATHER.

WITH characteristic inconsistency the Christian will exclaim " Here is another blasphemous title. What has God to do with the weather? " Everything, sir. Not a sparrow falls to the ground without his knowledge, and do you think he fails to regulate the clouds? The hairs of your head are numbered, and do you think he cannot count the rain-drops? Besides, your clergy pray for a change in the weather when they find it necessary; and to whom do they pray but God? True, they are getting chary of such requests, but the theory is not disavowed, nor can it be unless the Bible is discarded as waste-paper; and the forms of supplication for rain and fine weather still remain in the Prayer Book, although many parsons must feel like the parish clerk who asked " What's the use of praying for rain with the wind in that quarter?"

We might also observe that as God is omnipotent he does everything, or at least everything which is not left (as parsons would say) to man's freewill, and clearly the weather is not included in that list. God is also omniscient, and what he foresees and does not alter is virtually his own work. Even if a tile drops on a man's head in a gale of wind, it falls, like the sparrow, by a divine rule; and it is really the Lord who batters the poor fellow's skull. An action for assault would undoubtedly lie, if there were any court in which the case could be pleaded. What a frightful total of damages would be run up against the defendant if every plaintiff got a proper verdict! For, besides all the injuries inflicted on mankind by "accident," which only means the Lord's malice or neglect, it is a solemn fact (on the Theist's hypothesis) that God has killed every man, woman, and child that ever died since the human race began. We are born here without being consulted, and hurried away without the least regard to our convenience.

But let us keep to the weather. A gentleman who was feeding the fish at sea heard a sailor singing "Britannia rules the waves." "Does she?" he groaned, "Then I wish she'd rule them straighter." Most of us might as fervently wish that the Lord ruled the weather better. Some parts of the world are parched and others flooded. In some places the crops are spoiled with too much sun, and in others with too little. Some people sigh for the sight of a cloud, and others people see nothing else. Occasionally a famine occurs in India which might have been averted by half our superfluity of water. Even at home the weather is always more or less of a plague. Its variation is so great that it is always a safe topic of conversation. You may go out in the morning with a light heart, tempted by the sunshine to leave your overcoat and umbrella at home; and in the evening you may return wet through, with a sensation in the nose that prognosticates a doctor's bill. You may enter a theatre, or a hall, with dry feet, and walk home through a deluge. In the morning a south wind breathes like zephyr on your cheeks, and in the evening your face is pinched with a vile and freezing north-easter.

"Oh," say the pious, "it would be hard to please everybody, and foolish to try it. Remember the old man and his ass." Perhaps so, but the Lord should have thought of that before he made us; and if he cannot give us all we want, he might show us a little consideration now and then. But instead of occasionally accommodating the weather to us, he invariably makes us accommodate ourselves to the weather. That is, if we can. But we cannot, at any rate in a climate like this. Men cannot be walking almanacks, nor carry about a wardrobe to suit all contingencies. In the long run the weather gets the better of the wisest and toughest, and when the doctors have done with us we head our own funeral procession. The doctor's certificate says asthma, bronchitis, pulmonary consumption, or something of that sort. But the document ought to read " Died of the weather."

Poets have sung the glory of snowy landscapes, and there is no prettier sight than the earth covered with a virgin mantle, on which the trees gleam like silver jewels. But what an abomination snow is in cities. The slush seems all the blacker for its whiteness, and the pure flakes turn into the vilest mud. Men and horses are in a purgatory. Gloom sits on every face. Pedestrians trudge along, glaring at each other with murderous eyes ; and the amount of swearing done is enough to prove the whole thing a beastly mistake.

It seems perfectly clear that when the Lord designed the weather, two or three hundred million years ago, he forgot that men would build cities. He continues to treat us as agriculturalists, even in a manufacturing and commercial country like this. Why should people get drenched in Fleet-street while the Buckinghamshire farmers want rain? The arrangement is obviously stupid. God Almighty ought to drop the rain and snow in the country, and only turn on enough water in the cities to flush the sewers. He ought also to let the rain fall in the night. During the daytime we want the world for our business and pleasure, and the Rain Department should operate when we are snug in bed. This is a reforming age. Gods, as well as men, must move on. It is really ridiculous for the Clerk of the Weather to be acting on the old lines when everybody down below can see they are behind the time. If he does not improve we shall have to agitate on the subject. Home Rule is the order of the day. We need Home for the globe, and we cannot afford to let the weather be included in the imperial functions. It is a domestic affair. And as the Lord has considerably mismanaged it, he had better hand it over to us, with full power to arrange it as we please.

MIRACLES.

What is a miracle? Some people would reply, an act of God. But this definition is far too wide. In the theistic sense, it would include everything that happens; and in the sense of our archaic bills of lading, it would include fire and shipwreck.

Others would reply, a miracle is a wonder. But this definition would include every new, or at least every surprising new fact. A black swan would have been a wonder before Australia was discovered, but it would have been no miracle. Railways, telegraphs, telephones, electric light, and even gas light, would be wonders to savages, yet neither are they miracles. One of the Mahdi's followers was astonished by an English officer, who pulled out his false eye, tossed it in the air, caught it, and replaced it; after which he asked the flabbergasted Arab whether his miraculous Mahdi could do that. It was a greater wonder than the Mahdi could perform; still it was not a miracle. Ice was so great a wonder to the King of Siam that he refused to credit its existence. Yet it was not miraculous, but a natural product, existing in practically unlimited quantities in the polar regions. We might multiply these illustrations *ad infinitum*, but what we have given will suffice. If not, let the reader spend an evening at Maskelyne and Cooke's, where he will see plenty of startling wonders and not a miracle amongst them.

Hume's definition of a miracle as a violation of a law of nature, is the best ever given, and it really is as perfect as such a definition can be. It has been carped at by Christian scribblers, and criticised by superior theologians like Mozley. But, to use Mr. Gladstone's phrase, it keeps the field. Even the criticisms of Mill and Huxley leave its merit unimpaired. The ground taken by these is, that to say a miracle is a violation of a law of nature is to prejudge the question, and to rule out all future facts in the interest of a prepossession. Mill, however, allows that a miracle is a violation of a valid induction, and as a law of nature means nothing more it is difficult to understand why he takes any exception to Hume's statement of the case. It is perfectly obvious that Hume's argument is not metaphysical, but practical. He does not discuss the *possibility* but the *probability* of miracles. He reduces the dispute to a single point, namely, whether the person who relates a miracle (for to the world at large the question is necessarily one of testimony) is deceived or deceiving, or whether the otherwise universal experience of mankind is to be disbelieved; in other words, whether he or the rest of the world is mistaken. One man may, of course, be right, and all the human race opposed to him wrong, but time will settle the difference between them. That *time*, however, simply means general experience through long ages; and that is precisely the tribunal which Hume's argument appeals to.

Quarrelling with Hume's definition is really giving up miracles altogether, for, except as supernatural evidence, they are no more important than shooting stars. The very nature of a miracle, in whatever formula it may be expressed, is superhuman, and having a purpose, it is also supernatural; in other words, it is a special manifestation of divine power for a particular object. Whether, being so, it is a violation, a contravention, or a suspension of the laws of nature, is a mere question about words.

We may say that a miracle has three elements. It is first a fact, unaccountable by science; secondly, it requires a conscious agent; and thirdly, it results from the exercise of a power which that agent does not naturally possess.

Let us descend to illustration. Huxley takes the following case. Suppose the greatest physiologist in Europe alleged that he had seen a centaur, a fabulous animal, half man and half horse. The presumption would be that he was laboring under hallucination; but if he persisted in the statement he would have to submit to the most rigorous criticism by his scientific colleagues before it could be believed; and everybody would feel sure beforehand that he would never pass through the ordeal successfully. The common experience, and therefore the common sense, of society would be dead against him, and probably he would be refused the honor of examination even by the most fervid believers in ancient miracles.

But after all the centaur, even if it existed, would not be a miracle, but a monstrosity. It does not contain the three elements we have indicated. Real miracles would be of a different character. Plenty may be found in the Bible, and we may make a selection to illustrate our argument. Jesus Christ was once at a marriage feast, when the wine ran short, which was perhaps no uncommon occurrence. Being of a benevolent turn of mind, and anxious that the guests should remember the occasion, he turned a large quantity of cold water into fermented juice of the grape. Now water contains oxygen and hydrogen in definite proportions, and nothing else, while wine contains in addition to these, carbon and other elements, being in fact a very complex liquid. Jesus Christ must, therefore, in turning water into wine, have created something, and that transcends human power. Here, then, we have a complete miracle, according to Hume's definition and our own theory.

We do not say the miracle never occurred, although we no more believe in it than we believe the moon is made of green cheese. We are willing to regard it as susceptible of proof. But does the proof exist? To answer this we must inquire what kind of proof is necessary. An extraordinary story should be supported by extraordinary evidence. It requires the concurrent and overwhelming testimony of eye-witnesses. We must be persuaded that there is no collusion between them, that none of them has anything to gain by deception, that they had no previous tendency to expect such a thing, and that it was practically impossible that they could be deluded. Now let any man or any Christian seriously ask himself whether the evidence for Jesus Christ's miracle is of this character. Four evangelists write his life, and only one mentions the occurrence. Even he was certainly not an eye-witness, nor does he pretend to be, and the weight of evidence is against his gospel having been written till long after the first disciples of Jesus were dead. But even if the writer distinctly declared himself an eye-witness, and if it were undeniable that he lived on the spot at the time, his single unsupported testimony would be absurdly inadequate to establish the truth of the miracle. Every reader will at once see that the established rules of evidence are not conformed to, and whoever accepts the miracle must eke out reason with faith.

So much for the evidence of miracles. Their intellectual or moral value is simply nil. The greatest miracle could not really convince a man of what his reason condemned ; and if a prophet could turn water into wine, it would not necessarily follow that all he said was true. In fact, truth does not require the support of miracles ; it flourishes better without their assistance. Universal history shows that miracles have always been employed to support falsehood and fraud, to promote superstition, and to enhance the profit and power of priests.

A REAL MIRACLE.*

It is a common belief among Protestants, though not among Catholics, that the age of miracles is past. For a long time it has been very difficult to find a real case of special providence. There are stories afloat of wonderful faith-cures, and the followers of John Wesley, as well as the followers of William Booth, often shake their heads mysteriously, and affect to trace the hand of God in certain episodes of their experience. But such cases are too personal, and too subjective, to challenge criticism or inquiry. Investigating them is like exploring a cloud. There is nothing tangible for the mind to seize, nothing to stand by as the basis of discussion. What is wanted is a real objective miracle, a positive *fact*. Happily such a miracle has come to the aid of a distressed Christianity; it is worth tons of learned apologetics, and will give "the dying creed" a fresh lease of life.

Unfortunately the world at large is in gross ignorance of this astonishing event. Like the earthquake, the eclipse, and the wholesale resurrection of saints at the crucifixion of Christ, it has excited very little public attention. But this dense apathy, or Satanic conspiracy of silence, must not be allowed to hide a precious truth. We therefore do our best to give it publicity, although in doing so we are blasting our own foundations; for we belong to a party which boasts that it seeks for truth, and we are ready to exclaim, "Let truth prevail though the heavens fall."

Most of our readers will remember the late accident on the Brighton line at Norwood. A bridge collapsed, and only the driver's presence of mind averted a great loss of life. Of course the driver did his obvious duty, and presence of mind is not uncommon

---

* May, 1891.

enough to be miraculous. But that does not exhaust the matter. The driver (Hargraves) is perfectly sure he received divine assistance. He is a man of pious habits. He never leaves his house without kneeling down with his wife and imploring God's protection. He never steps on the engine without breathing another prayer. On the morning of the accident his piety was in a state of unusual excitation. He begged his wife to "pray all that day"—which we presume she did, with intervals for refreshment; and he knelt down himself in the passage before opening his front door. When the accident happened he put the brake on and cried "Lord, save us," and according to the *Christian World* "it has since been stated by expert engineers that no train was ever before pulled up in such a short distance."

A carping critic might presume to ask the names and addresses of these "expert engineers." He might also have the temerity to inquire the precise distance in which the train was pulled up, the shortest distance in which other trains have been pulled up, and the weight and velocity of the train in each case. He might also meanly suggest that putting on the brake left as little as possible to Providence. For our part, however, we will not pursue such hypercriticism. It is applying to a miracle a test which it is not fitted to stand. Something must be left to faith, something must be reserved from reason, or the stoutest miracle would soon fall into a galloping consumption. The man in whom a pious disposition counteracts the restless play of thought, will not demand absolute proof; he will only require an encouraging amount of evidence; and he will dutifully lift his face and hands to heaven, exclaiming, "Lord I believe, help thou mine unbelief."

The line we shall follow is a different one. Without questioning the miracle, we venture to ask why it was not more complete. Lives were saved, but several persons were injured. Was this due to the fact that Hargraves' prayer was not sufficiently above proof? Did the Lord answer the prayer according to its insensity? Was there a sceptic in the train who partially neutralised its effect? Or did the Lord proceed on the method favored by priests, preventing the miracle from being too obvious, but giving the incident a slightly supernatural appearance, in order to confirm the faith of believers without convincing the callous sceptics, whose deep sin of incredulity places them beyond "the means of grace and the hope of glory?"

Nor are these questions exhaustive. Very much remains to be said. It appears that the Norwood bridge collapsed through a secret flaw in the iron-work. Could not the Lord, therefore, in answer to Hargraves' prayers—which surely extended to the interests of his employers—have inspired one of the Company's engineers with the notion of some unsoundness in the structure? This would have saved a good deal of property, and many passengers from suffering a shock whose effects may haunt them for years, and perhaps send them to untimely graves? Might not the Lord have cleared the roadway below, knocked down the bridge in the night, and brought some one to see the collapse who could have carried the tidings to the signalmen? Certainly there seems a remarkable want of subtlety in the ways of Providence. It looks as though the Deity heard a prayer now and then, and jerked out a bit of miracle in a more or less promiscuous manner.

What has happened to Providence since the Bible days? Miracles then were clear, convincing, and artistically rounded. You could not possibly mistake them for anything else. Baalam's ass, for instance, was not a performing "moke"; it does not appear to have known a single trick; and when it opened its mouth and talked in good Moabitish, the miracle was certain and triumphant. In the same way, the Norwood miracle might have been unadulterated with the usual operations of nature. The bridge might have collapsed as the train approached, driver Hargraves might have said his prayer, the train might have leapt across the chasm, picked up the connection on the other side, and pursued its way to Brighton as if nothing had happened. But as the case stands, Providence and the safety-brake act together, and it is difficult to decide their shares in the enterprise. Further, the miracle is sadly mixed. Any human being would have planned it better, and made it stand out clearly and firmly.

This Norwood miracle, however, seems the best obtainable in these days. It is a minute return for all the prayers of the clergy, to say nothing of pious engine-drivers; a miserable dividend on the gigantic investment in supernaturalism. We pity the poor shareholders, though we must congratulate the directors on the large salaries they draw from the business. We also pity poor old Providence, who seems almost played out. Once upon a time he was in fine form; miracles were as common as blackberries; Nature seldom got an innings, and Jehovah was all over the field. But nowadays Nature seems to have got the better of him. She scarcely leaves him a corner for his operations, and what little he does (if he does anything) has to be done in obscurity. Poor old Providence, we fancy, has had his day. His vigor is gone, his lively fancy has degenerated into moping ineptitude, the shouts of millions of worshippers cannot stimulate his sluggishness into any more effective display than this Norwood miracle. Most sincerely we offer him our condolence as the sleeping partner in the business of religion. By and bye we may offer our condolence to the active partners, the priests of all denominations, who still flourish on a prospectus which, if once true, is now clearly fraudulent. When their business dwindles, in consequence of a failing supply of good supernatural articles, they will only live on the price of actual deliveries, and a Norwood miracle will hardly afford six of them a mouthful apiece.

JESUS ON WOMEN.

"FOR religions," says Michelet, "woman is mother, tender guardian, and faithful nurse. The gods are like men; they are reared, and they die, upon her bosom." Truer words were never uttered. Michelet showed in *La Sorcière*, from which this extract is taken, as well as in many other writings, that he fully understood the fulcrum of priestcraft and the secret of superstition. Women are everywhere the chief, and in some places the only, supporters of religion. Even in Paris, where Freethinkers abound, the women go to church and favor the priest. Naturally, they impress their own views on the children, for while the father's influence is fitful through his absence from home, the mother's is constant and therefore permanent. Again and again the clergy have restored their broken power by the hold upon that sex which men pretend to think the weaker, although they are obviously the sovereigns of every generation. Men may resolve to go where they please, but if they cannot take the women with them they will never make the journey. Women do not resist progress, they simply stand still, and by their real, though disguised, rule over the family, they keep the world with them. Freethinkers should look this fact in the face. Blinking it is futile. Whoever does that imitates the hunted ostrich, who does not escape his doom by hiding his head. The whole question lies in a nutshell. Where one sex is, the other will be; and there is a terrible, yet withal a beautiful, truth in the upshot of Mill's argument, that if men do not lift women up, women will drag men down. In the education and elevation of women, then, lies the great hope of the future. Leading Freethinkers have always seen this. Shelley's great cry, " Can man be free if woman be a slave?" is one witness, and Mill's great essay on *The Subjection of Women* is another.

Go where you will, you find the priests courting the women. They act thus, not because they despise men, or fear them, but because they (often unconsciously) feel that when they have captured the " weaker " sex, the other becomes a speedy prey. Perhaps a dim perception of this truth hovered in the minds of those who composed the story of the Fall. The serpent does not bother about Adam. He just makes sure of Eve, and she settles her " stronger " half. Milton makes Adam reluct and wrangle, but it is easy to see he will succumb to his wife's persuasions. He swears he won't eat, but Eve draws him all the time with a silken string, mightier than the biggest cable.

When the Christian monks were proselytising at Rome, they were hated, says Jortin, " as beggarly impostors and hungry Greeks who seduced ladies of fortune and quality." Hated, yes; but what did the hatred avail? The women were won, and the game was over. Men growled, but they had to yield. The same holds good to-day. Watch the congregations streaming out of church, count ten bonnets to one hat, and you might fancy Christianity played out because the men stay at home and neglect its ministrations. Nothing of the sort. Men may desert the churches as they like, but while the women go the clergy are safe. Examine the church and chapel organisations closely, and you will see how nine-tenths of everything is designed for women and children. Yes, the bonnet is the priest's talisman. Like Constantine's legendary cross, it bears the sign *By this Conquer*.

On the other hand, the clergy never fail to remind women that religion is their best friend. Without our doctrines and our holy Church, they say, there would be social chaos; the wild passions of men would spurn control, marriage would be despised, wives would become mistresses, homes would disappear, and children would be treated as encumbrances. There is not a grain of truth in this, for religion has fomented, countenanced, or cloaked, more sensuality and selfishness than it has ever repressed. But it is a powerful appeal to woman's healthy domestic sentiment. She feels, if she does not know, that marriage is her sheet-anchor, and the home an ark on a weltering flood. When the priest tells her that religion is the surety of both, he plucks at her heart, which vibrates to its depths, and she regards him as her savior.

Historically, the Christian religion, at least, has never been woman's real friend. It claims credit for everything; but what has it achieved? Monogamy was practised by the rude Teutons before Christianity "converted" them by fraud and force, and it was the law in pagan Greece and Rome before the Christian era. Yet in the Bible there is not a word against polygamy. God's favorites had as many wives as they could manage, and Solomon had enough to manage *him*. In the New Testament there is only one man who is told to be "the husband of one wife," and that is a bishop. Even in *his* case, a facetious sceptic hints, and the Mormons argue, that the command only means that he must have *one wife at least*.

There are two supreme figures in the New Testament, Paul and Jesus. What Paul says about women I will deal with presently. For the moment I confine myself to Jesus. Let the reader remember that Christianity cannot transcend the Bible, any more than a stream can rise above its source.

Like most revivalists and popular preachers, Jesus had a number of women dangling at his heels, but his

teaching on the subject in hand is barren, or worse.
As a child, he gave his mother the slip at Jerusalem,
and caused her much anxiety. During his minstry, when
his mother and his brethren wished to speak with him,
he forgot the natural ties of blood, and coolly remarked
that his family were those who believed his gospel.
On another occasion he roughly said to Mary,
"Woman, what have I to do with thee?" These
examples are not very edifying. If Christ is our
great exemplar, the fashion he set of treating his
nearest relatives is "more honored in the breach than
in the observance."

Jesus appears to have despised the union of the
sexes, therefore marriage, and therefore the home. He
taught that in heaven, where all are perfect, there is
neither marrying nor giving in marriage; the saints
being like angels, probably of the neuter gender. In
Matthew xix. 12 he appears to recommend emascula-
tion, praising those who make themselves "eunuchs for
the kingdom of heaven's sake." This doctrine is too
high for flesh and blood, but Origen and other early
Christians practised it literally. We may be sure that
those who trample on manhood have no real respect
for womanhood. Hence the Romish Church has
always praised up virginity, which is simply an
abnegation of sex. Cruden shrinks from the literal
sense of Christ's words, and says that the "eunuchs"
he refers to are those who "upon some religious motive
do abstain from marriage and the use of all carnal
pleasures; that they may be less encumbered with the
cares of the world, and may devote themselves more
closely to the service of God." Moonshine! Origen
was a better judge than Cruden. If Jesus did not
mean what he said, why did he take the trouble to
speak? His doctrine is that of the anchorite. It led
naturally to the filthy wretches, called monks, who
dreaded the sight of a woman, and hoped to please God
by stultifying nature. It also led to the Church law
forbidding women to touch the sacrament with their

naked hands, lest they should pollute it. Only women who relish that infamous law can feel any respect for the teaching of Jesus.

PAUL ON WOMEN.

CHRISTIANITY, as the centuries have revealed its practical character, owes more to Paul than to Jesus. Its dogmas are mostly derived from the epistles of the great apostle. Many a true believer thinks he is obeying the carpenter's son, when all the time he is obeying the Tarsus tent-maker. The Christian road to heaven was laid out and paved, not by Jesus himself, but by the gentleman he (or a sunstroke) converted outside Damascus.

Paul was in some respects a better teacher than Jesus. He was more practical, and with all his misty metaphysics he had a firmer hold on the realities of life. But with respect to women, he follows dutifully in his Savior's wake, and elaborates, rather than supplements, the sexual injunctions we have already dealt with. Like his Master, he looks down upon marriage, and is evidently of opinion that if men should not make themselves eunuchs they should live as such. The American Shakers are only carrying out his policy in this respect. If all the world imitated them the human race would soon expire. It would then be impossible to adopt the children of outsiders, families would be gradually extinguished, and the second coming of Christ would be prematurely hastened.

Paul was a bachelor, and a crusty one. According to tradition or calumny, he was jilted by a Jewish woman, and this may account for his peevish attitude towards the sex. In the seventh chapter of the first of Corinthians he gives vent to a great deal of nasty nonsense. "It is good," he says, "for a man not to touch a woman." If he had meant by this that men were not to thrash their wives we should have thoroughly agreed with him. But what he means is that there should be no sexual intercourse. He was especially severe on young widows who contemplated a second marriage. No doubt if he had seen a young widow whose weeds, as is generally the case, were arranged coquettishly, he would have muttered "Anathema Maranatha." As his own constitution was liable to occasional weaknesses, he might have added, "Get thee behind me, Satan."

A few verses later he expresses himself with greater clearness than Jesus Christ ever attained to: "I say therefore to the unmarried and widows, It is good for them if they abide even as I. But if they cannot contain, let them marry; for it is better to marry than to burn." Paul wished the same end as Jesus. He desired to see every person celibate, but having a little more common sense than Jesus, he saw that such preaching would never be extensively practised (especially by young widows) and he was obliged to make a concession to human frailty. The very fact, however, shows that his view of the question was radically wrong. Marriage is not an excusable weakness, but the normal condition of mankind. Physiologically, mentally, and morally this truth holds good. Even the highest virtues have never sprung from monasteries and convents, but from the rude rough world of toiling and suffering men and women outside.

According to Paul, although marriage was lawful, virginity was a higher state; that is, to be perfect, a woman must stultify her nature and trample upon her maternal instincts. It also implies that she is essentially impure, and that she can only please God by abnegating her sex. This is the deepest disrespect of womanhood, as every healthy wife and mother would admit if such stuff were taught by another than Paul.

The great apostle troubled his poor head about the heads of women. If he lived now when the ladies affect short hair he would go raving mad. It was a subject on which he felt profoundly. To his mind a woman losing her long hair, was like an angel falling from glory. He warns the whole sex against meddling with their tresses. Men, however, are recommended to crop close, long hair being " shameful." We have a shrewd suspicion that Paul was bald. Perhaps if hair restorer had been then invented a successful trial might have considerably changed his views upon this subject.

Man was not created for woman, says Paul, but woman for man. He is of course alluding to the old Rib Story. But a similar observation would have been as sensible about the two halves of a pair of scissors. When they meet what does it matter which was made for the other? Consistently with this view he says, " Wives, submit yourselves unto your own husbands as unto the Lord . . . as the Church is subject unto Christ so let the wives be to their husbands in everything." Some men have tried this with no great success, and many a man thinks he is having his own way " in everything " when he is sweetly and beautifully led by the nose. Obedience is a hateful word in marriage. Its introduction makes the wife a legalised concubine. Besides, if there *must* be obedience, Paul's rule is ridiculously sweeping, for some women have more sense and judgment than their husbands. Every afflicted woman who applies to the magistrate for relief from the sot who curses her home is flying in the face of Paul. " My dear woman," the magistrate *should* say, " your request is very reasonable, but it is very unorthodox. Go home and read the fifth chapter of Ephesians, where you will see that wives must obey their husbands in *everything*."

Paul (1 Cor. xiv. 34, 35; Tim. ii. 11, 12) warns women to keep silence in church, for " it is not permitted unto them to speak." Having written this line,

Paul must have got up and strutted round the room like a ruffled cock. "Let the woman," he says, "learn in silence with all subjection. I suffer not a woman to teach, nor to usurp authority over the man, but to be in silence." Hear, hear! from the males in the body of the synagogue. Evidently Paul could bray on occasion as lustily as Balaam's ass. If the women "will learn anything," which he clearly thought problematical, "let them ask their husbands at home." Fancy some women with no other sources of information!

The reason Paul gives for woman's inferiority is that Mrs. Eve was first tempted by the serpent. And a capital thing too! If Mrs. Eve had not eaten that apple the human race would still number two, or else, if none of them died, they would be thicker than barrelled herrings.

Our Church of England marriage service follows the teaching of Paul. While the husband promises to love the wife, the wife promises to love, honor and obey the husband. Many ladies say these words at the altar with a mental reservation. When they are obliged to do this they tacitly admit that Paul and the Church are wrong. But if so the Bible is wrong. The fact is that the "blessed book," instead of being woman's best friend, is her worst enemy. The Tenth Commandment makes her domestic property, and Paul winds up by telling her that her sole duty is to play second fiddle in a minor key.

MOTHER'S RELIGION.

RELIGION is the feminine element in human nature. Science is the masculine. One accepts, the other inquires; one believes, the other proves; one loves the old, the other the new; one submits, the other dares; one is conservative, and the other progressive.

I say this with no disrespect to women. Evolution has made them what they are, and evolution will remake them. Nor do I slight the noble band of advanced women, the vanguard of their sex, who have shed a lustre on our century. I merely take a convenient metaphor, which crystallises a profound truth, though fully conscious of its shortcomings and exclusions.

Woman is still the citadel of religion. Thither the priest flies from the attacks of scepticism. There he finds an inviolable refuge. The mother, the wife, the sister, shield him and his creed; and their white arms and soft eyes are a better guard than all the weapons in the armory of his faith. His are the coward's tactics, but all creatures—even priests—plead the necessity of living, and have the artful instinct of self-preservation.

Religious by inheritance and training, woman rears her children for the Church. Spiritual as well as bodily perils shake her prophetic soul as she peers into the future through the eyes of the child upon her knee. She whispers of God with accents of awe, that fall solemnly on the little one's mind. She trains the knee to bend, the hands to meet in prayer, and the eyes to look upward. She wields the mighty spell of love, and peoples the air of life with phantoms. Infantile logic knows those dear lips cannot lie, and all is truth for all is love. Alas! the lesson has to come that the logic is faulty, that goodness may be leagued with lies, that a twisted brain may top the sweetest heart.

But long ere the lesson is learnt—if it *is* learnt—the mischief has been wrought. The child has been moulded for the priest, and is duly burnished with catechisms and stamped with dogmas. And how often, when the strong mind grows and bursts its bonds, when the mental eyes wax strong and see the falsehood, the mother's hand, through the child's training, plucks the life back from the fulfilment of its promise. How often, also, when the vigorous manhood has swept aside all illusions, there comes at length the hour of lassitude, and as the mother's voice steals through the caverns of memory the spectres of faith are startled from their repose.

Priests are always warning men against deserting the creed of their mothers. And even a *savant*, like Professor Gazzia, who writes on Giordano Bruno, knows the trick of touching this facile cord of the human heart. Speaking of Bruno's philosophy, he says: "I call it plainly the Negation of God, of that God, I mean, of whom I first heard *at my mother's knee.*"

But Freethinking mothers—and happily there are such—will use their power more wisely; and, above all, will not shrink from their duty. They have the fashioning of the young life—a transcendent privilege, with an awful responsibility. They will see that love nurtures the affections without suborning the intellect; that the young mind is encouraged to think, instead of being stuffed with conclusions; and they will some day find their exceeding rich reward. Their children, trained in the school of self-respect and toleration, will be wiser than the pupils of faith; and the bonds of love will be all the tenderer and stronger for the perception that the free individuality of the child's life was never sacrificed to the parent's authority.

BY THE SAME AUTHOR.

Crimes of Christianity. Vol. I. [Written in conjunction with J. M. Wheeler]. Hundreds of exact references to Standard Authorities. No pains spared to make it a complete, trustworthy, final, unanswerable Indictment of Christianity
  Chapters:—1, Christ to Constantine; 2, Constantine to Hypatia; 3, Monkery; 4, Pious Forgeries; 5, Pious Frauds; 6, Rise of the Papacy; 7, Crimes of the Popes; 8, Persecution of the Jews; 9, The Crusades. Cloth, gilt, 216pp., 2s. 6d.

Bible Handbook for Freethinkers and Inquiring Christians. [Edited in conjunction with W. P. Ball.] Complete, paper covers, 1s. 4d. Superior edition on superfine paper, bound in cloth, 2s.

Bible Heroes. Cloth, 2s. 6d.

The Grand Old Book. A Reply to the Grand Old Man. An Exhaustive answer to the Right Hon. W. E. Gladstone's "Impregnable Rock of Holy Scripture." 1s. Bound in cloth, 1s. 6d.

Christianity and Secularism. Four Nights' Public Debate with the Rev. Dr. James McCann. 1s. Superior edition, cloth, 1s. 6d

Darwin on God. 6d. Superior edition, cloth, 1s.

Infidel Death-Beds. Second edition, much enlarged, 8d. On superfine paper, in cloth, 1s. 3d.

Reminiscences of Charles Bradlaugh. 6d.

Comic Sermons and Other Fantasias. 8d.

Letters to the Clergy. *First Series.* 128pp. 1s.

A Defence of Free Speech. Three Hours' Address to the Jury before Lord Coleridge. With a Special Preface and many Footnotes. 4d.

Rome or Atheism—the Great Alternative. 3d.

Letters to Jesus Christ. 4d.

Philosophy of Secularism. 3d.

Atheism and Morality. 2d.

My Resurrection. A Missing Chapter from the Gospel of Matthew. 2d.

The Folly of Prayer. 2d.

Ingersollism Defended against Archdeacon Farrar. 2d.

Was Jesus Insane? A searching inquiry into the mental condition of the Prophet of Nazareth. 1d.

Christianity and Progress. A Reply to Mr. Gladstone. 2d.

The Impossible Creed. An Open Letter to Bishop Magee on the Sermon on the Mount. 2d.

What Was Christ? A Reply to J. S. Mill. 2d.

R. Forder, 28 Stonecutter-street, London, E.C.

www.ingramcontent.com/pod-product-compliance
Lightning Source LLC
Chambersburg PA
CBHW031813230426
43669CB00009B/1121